FUNCTIONAL AND FUNDED

Securing Your Nonprofit's Assets From The Inside-Out

HARVEY B. CHESS

PUBLISHER Harvey B. Chess

COVER
DESIGNER Patrick Hruby
Anya Farquhar

ISBN 978-0-9963147-1-8

Harvey B. Chess
Little River, California
FUNCTIONALANDFUNDED.COM

For those champions dedicated to
the success of community members for
and with whom they built a nonprofit.

TABLE OF CONTENTS

Forwarded Forward

The above play on words is because what follows decorated the predecessor to the book you now have before you. I was so pleased by it then—coming from a published author and man who has dedicated much of his life's work to the nonprofit sector—that it seems every bit appropriate this time around as well.

For the better part of forty years, Harvey Chess has reviewed, parsed, written, edited, shredded, rebuilt and otherwise put his fingerprints on more grant proposals than any other person on this planet. Period. Full stop.

In training sessions in every nonprofit setting imaginable, and in cities large and tiny, Harvey has honed an approach to successful grant proposal writing that often surprises people at first.

Harvey doesn't teach fundraising. The nonprofit landscape is littered with expensive books and training sessions claiming, usually unsuccessfully, to do that. Harvey's clear-headed approach is to help us understand and articulate how and why our projects and organizations benefit a constituency.

Armed with this, the nonprofit can approach a funding source as a potential partner: how the funding source with its money and the nonprofit organization with its expertise can form a partnership to alleviate a problem. Harvey Chess has tested this philanthropic partnership thousands of times, and it works.

I first met Harvey Chess when we both were trainers with the Grantsmanship Center in Los Angeles. Harvey was seldom in Los Angeles, however; he loved being in the field: Bangor, Maine; Elmira, New York; Window Rock, Arizona, and Juneau, Alaska, to name a few stops. Over the years, Harvey captivated his participants and me with his logic, his street savvy, his humor and his eloquent (occasionally grandiloquent) turn of phrase. Later in our careers, I was lucky enough to have Harvey as one of my senior program officers at the California Community Foundation in Los Angeles. There he spent almost a decade providing millions of dollars in project grants.

The book you are holding contains a no-nonsense and easily understood method of attracting assets to your nonprofit organization. It will make you laugh and more importantly, it will make you think. You are in for a treat.

JACK SHAKELY

President Emeritus, California Community Foundation Senior Fellow, Center on Philanthropy and Public Policy, University of Southern California

Author's Foreword

This writer readily admits not knowing what he was getting into when he stumbled through a door in 1965 and a recruiter for a new federal agency beguiled him by stating that the organization's mission was to eliminate poverty in this country.

Duly impressed—and amazed—I became a career-conditional employee of the Chicago Regional Office of the Federal Office of Economic Opportunity (RIP), actively involved in helping to create and fund local Community Action Agencies.

Didn't stick around because an offer to do some learn-as-I-went urban neighborhood organizing popped up—where, somehow we managed to get a neighborhood center up and running.

Then there was the job that followed with a local agency of the type we had started with federal funds. That's where I became immersed in going after resources, especially grants that were plentiful then.

And, as the branches on my tree of experience since those heady days reveal, I've gotten to continue working with and among people in nonprofit organizations as a much-traveled trainer, peripatetic consultant, and fitful volunteer.

I count these experiences as a rare privilege because they made possible consonance between the core values I have come to embrace and my work since then.

Much of my experience has been couched in the ever-alluring arena of grantseeking. Following years as a trainer with The Grantsmanship Center, I designed and delivered a well-received workshop for people seeking resources for nonprofit organizations all over the country.

Rounded out my experience within the nonprofit sector by once again jumping over to the giving side of the business, interacting both as a staff member and consultant with several grantmaking foundations.

So, I bring a well-done perspective to my newest endeavor as an author. What I've come to learn, practice and cherish are now embodied by my words in this book.

And, as for the book, what's important is my marrow belief that your nonprofit will tangibly benefit—on two levels—when you embrace and use the potent framework at its core to develop your resource-funding proposals. And, more will be revealed...

Finally, here, you should know that, yes, this book is about how to do what is needed to excel in going after resources for your nonprofit; but it offers you nothing like a *by-the-numbers formula* for doing so. This is because its author believes the book is far more important in first guiding you to think and communicate about how to do what's needed before you get around to proposing as much.

CHAPTER ONE

WHERE TO

Putting the Why before the How — centering your mission on impact, not projects

The spirit of this book is derived from the time- honored value of nonprofit organizations helping people respond to challenges to the quality of their lives—especially those organizations whose people take seriously the principles articulated in the following article from the Industrial Areas Foundation, titled Standing for the Whole:

> *"We believe in what we call the iron rule: never do for others what they can do for themselves. Never. This rule, difficult to practice consistently, sometimes violated, is central to our view of the nature of education, of leadership, of effective organizing. This cuts against the grain of some social workers and program peddlers who try to reduce people and families to clients, who probe for needs and lacks and weaknesses, not strength and drive, not vision and values, not democratic and entrepreneurial initiative. The iron rule implies that the most valuable and enduring form of development—intellectual, social, political—is the development people freely choose and fully own."*

These values are no less important when nonprofit organizations engage in the ever-present necessity of pursuing diversified resources to allow them to keep on keeping on. Discussing this in detail forms the substance of this book, but before getting to this, let's consider a couple of persistent traits among nonprofit organizations that prop up a perverse form of business as usual. And, as you will see, this book is not about business as usual.

To begin, when attempting to convince others to support our organizations we, in effect, convey that they should do so because we run excellent programs. As reasonable as this might appear, there is a damning corollary that accompanies such an approach. Rather than focusing on the people for whom our organization was created in the first place, we emphasize an array of proposed activities. A mania for process, emblematic of a busy organization, replaces a proper concern for the quality of people's lives, the marker of a legitimate organization.

Another enduring characteristic of this form of nonprofit business-as-usual also contributes to the obsession with program delivery. **This is the tendency for nonprofits to botch their mission statements.** The basis for this assertion is unassailable when bearing in mind that nonprofits are often described as public benefit organizations. So, the only legitimate mission for a such a nonprofit is its own version of the public benefit of helping people improve the quality of their lives. Period.

But, against this standard, a seemingly unending procession of statements emerges describing the activities an organization carries out as its mission, or, at best, activities proposed to lead up to some form of impact. Once again process overrides payoff. Take a look at three real-life examples.

> *Our mission is to provide effective educational and supportive services to maximize the strengths of individuals and build resilient communities.*
>
> *Our mission is to build local collaborations to support local arts organizations.*
>
> *Our mission is to deliver highest quality healthcare services.*

how your organization works.

In every instance we find an organization asserting that its purpose is, first and foremost, to be active rather than effective. Even when impact is specified, as in the second example, the proposed activities precede it as the essence of the mission. Small wonder, with mission statements such as these, that so many nonprofits base their arguments for continuing on an inward-looking devotion to program delivery.

The end result of what has to be considered a myopic approach to front and center a nonprofit organization is akin to a stale sense of stasis. This is typified by the many proposals that request support to an ongoing program, that is, funding more of the same, with perhaps the insinuation of more neediness thrown into the mix. It need not be this way, nor should it be.

So, changing an organization's mission statement to emphasize external impact rather than internal process is a step in the right direction. Let's recast the previous examples accordingly.

> *Our mission is to help individuals maximize their strengths and to contribute to building resilient communities by providing them with effective educational and supportive services.*
>
> *Our mission is to help local arts organizations thrive as community resources by building local coalitions.*
>
> *Our mission is to achieve optimal community health and save lives by delivering highest quality healthcare services.*

Making these simple twists is profoundly important because each one represents shifting an organization's emphasis to that of fostering success among its folks before describing how to do this.

The ultimate measure of any nonprofit's relevance and the basis by which it should be evaluated is the extent to which it can document the impact of its work rather than simply having carried it out. **Think about it.**

And think about this simple but profound shift as setting up and leading into business as unusual when you seek assets for your nonprofit organization. This leads to the potent tactics and strategies of such an approach that follow. Make these your own, and you'll be able to represent your organization as enterprising, resilient and respectable—along with presenting far more convincing proposals for its support in a crowded, competitive marketplace for resources. Equally important, you will strengthen your organization by virtue of the way you develop these proposals.

Effective mission statements elevate

CHAPTER TWO

THREE

How to realize the full potential of funding proposals

- *Proposals as craft*
- *Storytelling that adapts*
- *Progress through broader focus*

Even when approaching the business of resource development from a different angle, business as unusual we're calling it, the written funding proposal remains fundamentally and incontestably prominent. As such, here are three critical factors to consider as they relate to your grasp of creating and using your own proposal.

1. Proposals as craft

First, my own efforts writing proposals and my work with nonprofit proposal writers for years confirm that the skills needed to write effectively and successfully remain elusive. This predicament alone is enough to suggest why you have this book in front of you. As you read, dog-ear and re-read it, you'll discover how to strengthen the way you visualize, develop and use these skills.

We need to embrace such skills here and now. We need to improve the quality of our work in that teeming resource marketplace when reaching out to fortify the pursuit of our organizations' missions. This in itself constitutes a substantial challenge, but it doesn't stop there—there is even more complexity to consider when pursuing resources to energize our nonprofits.

2. Storytelling that adapts

This becomes clear as the second factor to influence your work when you realize that what was formerly largely confined to grantseeking presently amounts to much more. The best word to describe what confronts the resource-seeking

YOUR NONPROFIT'S ENGINE

Each component can generate
the assets to fuel your mission.

nonprofit is flux, as the preceding diagram to guide your efforts to build organizational assets illustrates.

Take a look at the broad possibilities that surface within your Nonprofit's Engine. You might find yourself with the opportunity to create any number of the following options within your organization:

- *The well-planned proposal out-the-door, or the hastily conceived one when you learn of an imminent funder deadline*
- *The occasional opportunity to follow up the proposal you submitted with a sit-down meeting with funder reps*
- *The materials needed to respond to a social media funding opportunity*
- *The details to develop and submit your business plan, and/or your organization's long-range strategy*
- *The specifics to develop and embrace your organization's fundraising strategy*
- *The prospect of contemplating and preparing for a possible collaboration with another organization*
- *Copy for your direct mail solicitation*
- *Your part in a planned, face-to-face meeting with a prospective donor*
- *A presentation to convince one of the many civic organizations that spread resources around your community to include your nonprofit*

- *An impact during a chance meeting with a few moments to serve up your version of what is often called the elevator pitch*

- *A compelling story when interacting with media outlets to get them to highlight your outfit*

- *Public relations materials for broad dissemination*

Each one of these scenarios represents the opportunity to display your organization for examination by others, to tell your story. You may recall Marshall McLuhan's adage that the medium is the message. What confronts us in this ever-changing landscape for the pursuit of resources is the need to place your nonprofit's message in the media.

However, all the media and communications savvy you can muster to deal with this emerging environment won't mean much if there is no clearly understood basis for articulating your message. The medium you choose to exploit may change. So too may the circumstances where you attempt to capture attention and resources, but the message about your organization and its work needs to be strong and steadfast. The message matters prominently.

As you work across various domains to present your nonprofit, especially to seek resources, your efforts will benefit from the ability to do this from a perspective and position of strength and resilience of the organization in its natural or community setting—the place where it pursues its mission. This, in turn, will depend on the quality of your organization's people, leaders among them, to offer a vision of the interrelationships and dedication to community engagement needed to achieve the improved quality of life expressed in your mission statement. Your nonprofit isn't in business alone.

When it comes to convincing others to make a decision to place their resources within your outfit's grasp, it seems reasonable to imagine that prospects will improve when your folks—participants, beneficiaries, volunteers, board and staff members—are all able to:

- *Tell a compelling story about your organization's work consistently marked by the success of the people who participate in your programs,*
- *Tell that story well, the prospect of which is strengthened by relationships and connections your organization and its people have, so that the message is not an isolated one,*
- *And do so in a time when perseverance and creativity are needed to adapt your resource development to changing opportunities.*

No matter where you take it, the substance of your organization's message is of utmost importance. Accordingly, we circle back to the concept that a carefully built funding proposal serves as the basis for outreach you will do to engage the interest of others, particularly those with assets your nonprofit could put to good use.

3. Progress through broader focus

The third factor relates, not surprisingly, to another facet of the primacy of funding proposals. This affirms that the time-honored decision to develop such proposals for

YOUR PROPOSALS MEAN (A LOT)

You can make much more out of the business of seeking resources than just cobbling together a funding proposal.

resource-seeking affords us the opportunity to utilize the building process to strengthen our organizations simultaneously. You can make much more out of the business of seeking resources than just cobbling together a funding proposal. You will find this assertion forms much of the basis for the in-depth discussion of unifying organizational and resource development in *CHAPTER 6, BRINGING IT TO LIFE.*

To sum up and reaffirm: We need to build up our proposal development skills because their mastery is a work in progress; we need to acknowledge, with resilience, flexibility and strength, the changing environment for the pursuit of resources; and finally, we need to use our endless devotion to create funding proposals as a way to build our organizations as well.

Before specifically examining what makes sense when building the type of proposal that will prove consistently useful, let's see what's to be learned by taking a look at the broad realm where nonprofits customarily use and misuse proposals to go after resources.

CHAPTER THREE

TO THE CHALLENGE

Why it's worth the effort to improve your proposal process and some pointers on how to do this.

The process of pursuing funds likely involves a number of events, as we've seen, not the least of which is the creation of a written proposal. Let's consider how developing yours presents the opportunity to answer the question of why your organization should be funded. By any measure of common sense nothing seems more important than answering that question. In the most basic terms, here's how:

Within your proposal demonstrate that:

- *Our mission-driven organization is strong and effective, and enjoys support from the community in which it is active.*
- *Our organization pursues its mission by successfully helping the people for whom it exists resolve challenges to the quality of their lives,*
- *We accomplish this mission-driven work through carefully considered and developed efforts such as the one described herein.*
- *And, as always, we take responsibility for documenting the impact of the proposed effort to once again bring about change for the better.*

Since the foregoing are markers of an effective funding proposal, it is compelling to assert that each is also a marker of an effective nonprofit organization. Look at the four items again. In the contentious arena where nonprofits compete for attention and resources, wouldn't it strike you as advantageous if yours was viewed and judged in light of the characteristics just represented?

Given such a prospect, we'll move along and look into to how to use a process fundamental to nonprofit existence, the pursuit of resources, to strengthen your organization before and while it does the pursuing. This is possible because building proposals has the potential to reinforce organizational capacity and this, in turn, contributes to a fertile environment in which to create compelling proposals. The one nourishes the other in an unbroken circle.

So, let's add to the idea that we can derive uncommon value from nonprofit resource development by continuing to concentrate on the confluence of your organization and its proposals in the funding realm. Take the impulse to continue the work of one's nonprofit outfit, for instance.

The test of how to sustain our organizations is front and center in our collective thinking in the nonprofit sector these days. Acquiring grants consistently emerges as a preferred way to meet the challenge. It is not difficult to imagine why this is so when contemplating the following grant-eligible categories extracted from a Foundation Center publication.

annual campaigns	*building/renovation*
capital campaigns	*conferences/ seminars*
consulting services	*continuing support*
curriculum development	*debt reduction*
emergency funds	*endowment funds*
equipment	*exchange programs*
fellowships	*general/operating support*
internships	*land acquisition*
lectureships	*matching funds*

operating budgets
program development
research
seed money
technical assistance
professorships
publications
scholarship funds
special projects

By any reasonable reckoning, this holds out a tantalizing list of possibilities for funding, so it's understandable that nonprofits consider pursuing grants an alluring prospect. So, we'll stick with this theme for a while, but acknowledge two factors before continuing.

First, the persistent challenge for your organization is to fortify the appeal of pursuing these—or any—funding categories by augmenting grantseeking with non-grant resource development within a multifaceted resource development strategy.

And, as for the longstanding predominance of grantseeking, even when included in such a multifaceted framework as just suggested, we need to acknowledge that there's often a problem in the pursuing we do.

To make the point, we don't seem to realize that grantseeking, or mislabeled grant writing, is both **overrated** and **undervalued**. This is no contradiction in terms, and it is essential we use the imprint of each characteristic to shape our tactics for going after resources needed to operate our organizations. Take a look.

The overrated status of going after grants is immediately apparent when bearing in mind that **90% of the money available** for charitable purposes in the private, non-government sector comes from living individuals through the instruments they establish to facilitate their largesse while alive, and through wills to continue their giving after death.

This is the realm of face-to-face transactions, related tax-wise planned giving, and now perhaps reaching individuals through social media. This suggests the importance of personal relationships and may well include the Almighty Ask where somebody has to face a promising, prospective benefactor or the representative of such a person, and request money or consideration for money tendered in the future.

Along with such a person-to-person, face-to-face sit-down, a range of additional techniques exists to pry money away from individual givers. Among the possibilities: knocking on doors, using the telephone to call or message, exploiting email and social media contacts, placing currency/coin-drop cans in public settings, running fundraising events, securing fees from individuals for services rendered, selling merchandise, soliciting contributions through direct mail appeals, orchestrating GoFundMe campaigns, and producing income from retail operations patronized by individuals.

The point is that the potency of individual giving to support nonprofits is incontestable, and its prominence demands commensurate attention in our pursuit of resources—all the more so when considering what follows.

The remaining 10% of the money in the private, non-government giving sector comes from foundations, corporations, and grantmaking public charities. The possibilities these outfits offer for flexible and strategic funding are

Grant proposal writing is both

and

Only 10% of money that goes to charitable causes comes from grants, but the process of creating effective proposals is worthwhile beyond funding.

sufficiently attractive to render writing grant proposals sensible and important, something borne out by the year-to-year volume of them generated by nonprofits.

There are also inducements aplenty to pursue the significant level of support through grants made available in the federal/state/local governmental arena. But they come with the burdens of complexity and the need for compliance with bureaucratic stipulations, along with fierce competition. The proverbial red tape and sense of dependency that often come with a sizable government grant certainly take something away from the otherwise joyous proposition of obtaining this money.

Consider also that the annual federal legislative process that creates grant funding takes it away as well. Talk to someone who has drawn a grant-funded salary only to have it zeroed-out by the action of a legislative body to discover how breathtaking this aspect of life in a nonprofit organization can be. The power of this phenomenon was always evident when people showed up in my training programs, and let it be known they were scurrying for another grant to keep their jobs because the previous grant was not being renewed.

Such plaintive circumstances reinforce the immutable truth that grants are finite: They always go away someday. This realization should govern your resource development tactics, and make it apparent that diversifying your efforts beyond grants makes good sense.

Okay, so we've put grants in their place. However, bear in mind that the value of your efforts to create needed written proposals at any given time never slackens. So,

Grants should just be
one aspect of your funding
(and marketing) plan.
Think long-term.

the very same proposal you built when it made sense to pursue a grant will serve you admirably as a study guide to organize your pitch, for example, whenever and however you approach individuals for support. (More on developing this theme to follow, especially in *CHAPTER 6, BRINGING IT TO LIFE.*)

With this, we've arrived at the opportunity to look further into the previous assertion that nonprofits, in effect, undervalue grants and their pursuit.

To start, as long as your organization is unclear about why and how to go about seeking grants, the process is likely to be dicey. Ask yourself—how often do the people in your organization get together to discuss and agree on a systematic approach for pursuing resources? Isn't it more likely that the discussion of whether or not to pursue a grant begins when a Request for Proposals (RFP) drifts across someone's desk, or when someone has encountered a recent crowdfunding success story, suggesting that all that need be done is to mimic that situation?

Instead of then seeking clarity and confidence about the fit between what your organization does and what the funder wants, have you rather found yourselves scrambling to fit your organization's activities into the widely publicized priorities of a recently active grant maker—something suspiciously similar to chasing money?

Add to this an equally debilitating scenario where resource development in any guise is an exercise detached from just about everything else that takes place in-house —and consigned to the isolated, part-time endeavors of one individual. No surprise that some of these folks confess to having fragmented knowledge of their own organizations. Some have even been heard, in past training programs, relating that they scarcely know the chief executive for whom they toil, along with never having been allowed to attend a board meeting. And yet, they nonetheless confront unreasonable expectations to excel as resource developers in such a dysfunctional setting.

Then, as previously intimated, there are those nonprofits that hire outside (grant writing!) consultants to develop proposals, with very little internal communication about their efforts or input from those who would be affected by what they propose. Rationale? Let's leave it to the expert, while we go about our other more pressing, persistent program activities.

Taken together, these ill-advised tendencies reinforce the contention that seeking grant resources is, yes, undervalued. A preferable organizational stance for intelligent, productive, multifaceted resource development, including the pursuit of grants, begins by acknowledging that the writers of nonprofit organization proposals deserve to be taken seriously and supported by their colleagues. Theirs are serious jobs. Proposal writing is a central activity for any organization seriously seeking funds, and creates the opportunity to do some important internal organizational development.

So let's examine both the proposal writers' tasks and the environment in which they operate, remaining mindful of the often neglected objective of establishing conditions within nonprofit organizations to support their success.

The following homily from an obviously sharp operative puts matters into proper perspective:

> *"I've had to struggle with the dilemma many times—clarifying roles and responsibilities while working with different programs in a multi-service organization. I've found it useful to take the time, very early in the program development process, to clarify roles and tasks. Usually, I'll do a careful read of a Request for Proposals and begin to construct a detailed task-timeline for getting the program developed and the proposal done.*
>
> *Once that timeline is drafted, I use it to begin the development process with the program folks who are involved. That process of deciding who will do what tasks by when is a wonderful way of being very clear about roles and deadlines.*
>
> *As a grant proposal writer, I don't pretend to have expertise in different content areas. Many program people hope that we, as proposal writers, will simply take the RFP, closet ourselves for several weeks, and emerge with a coherent proposal. I'm clear with program folks that those days are over—most proposals require a collaborative planning process with multiple agencies in a community, demonstration of knowledge about best practices in a particular program area, and a program design that is specific to the content area. I've found the task-timeline process to be a useful tool in getting program people to understand their important role*

Creating

proposals

HAS THE POTENTIAL TO

of your

organization.

in designing the nuts and bolts of a program and in deciding program objectives. The strongest message one can convey is that the proposal writer doesn't have to live with the program design—program staff does."

A wise woman, she's got it right. Words to remember and precepts to consider. The fact that she saw fit to distinguish her responsibilities and to assertively share her wisdom reinforces and counteracts the image of nonprofits consigning grantseeking to their operational nether regions, tolerated as a necessary evil. Since this would also seem to confirm that such pursuits are, as previously asserted, undervalued, this raises the question of why your group bothers to do this if it doesn't try to do it well.

Why not begin with the premise that doing this well, to reemphasize a central theme of this book, will find your people or community members building personal and organizational capacity by immersing themselves in the process of securing resources. Approaching the work involved in seeking external resources in this spirit takes those involved in the internal deliberations and strategizing into the heart and soul of the organization, and strengthens an organization from the inside out.

As for seeking resources and doing this well, how about properly valuing grantseeking, an often preferred tactic, with the same intensity and intelligence that you presumably bring to your other operations. This calls for the prospect of considering how to define, perhaps redefine, how, why and when to go after resources and to be clear about who gets involved in a resultant, agreed-upon and intentional process, something we will discuss in greater deal in the next chapter.

For now, it's sufficient to continue to imagine how resource-developing proposal writers can best do what they need to do, while considering just exactly what this looks like, along with discussing the supportive environment in which they should be able to operate. Once again it is worth repeating, it makes sense to establish conditions within nonprofit organizations to support their success.

Let's take a moment to keep in mind that your nonprofit's approach to pursuing resources always involves the other side, the outfits with the goods we seek. Here's what two operatives over there have to offer about your relationship with them.

One grant maker points out that organizations pursuing his foundation's grants should understand that they are, in effect, asking to become agents of his foundation. Another advises that you, the proposal writer, should share with the grant reader what fits the profile the funder seeks.

In spite of the ostensible gravity of this advice, what these two are recommending for a grantseeking organization is wondrously misguided.

Taking into consideration the importance of owning your proposal (more details to follow) and what it entails, you should never develop a proposal seeking resources solely based on the specifications overlaid by a prospective funder. There's no reason to imagine this will contribute to an environment where the people at the heart of your nonprofit will benefit from a resultant program effort. Nor should you allow your organization to become an automaton to some other entity just because it waves around the prospect of getting some money.

Connecting with and adapting to the imperatives of an external funder without qualification will prove futile, even if you get funded, unless you don't care a whit about why your organization exists in the first place. Parroting back what you think a funder wants to read can look like you're just chasing money.

A far better alternative, worth emphasizing, is to make certain you mark the process of seeking external resources by clearly understanding that this should always be couched in the sanctity of your mission and your persistence in making progress to complete that mission in all your efforts.

Taking the wisdom just imparted into consideration, let's circle back to the person in the middle of all this resource development action, the one who is responsible for hatching proposals. My experience now and then as one of these types, and among those who share such responsibilities, strongly suggests the need to perform as internal consultants rather than independent practitioners when a decision is made to solicit external resources. This finds us doing front-end work in our organization and community, and facilitating necessary communications before any writing comes into play.

This will mean jockeying for time with always-busy staff members and the people with whom they work. Here's how the mini-psychodrama might go.

STAFFER:
"I don't have time to meet with you. Didn't we hire you to write our proposals?"

YOU/INTERNAL CONSULTANT:
"You've got all the time you're going to get. Your choosing to give me some will bear on our ability to secure needed resources so you can keep doing your work—sit down."

The proposal writer's skill set doesn't stop with being a resourceful internal consultant. The inside work leading to development of a proposal necessarily leads to identifying where it will be delivered for consideration. This may be evident when your outfit chooses to respond to RFPs or Notices of Funding Availability sent in your direction by proactive funding sources. Bear in mind, however, that **most funding organizations do not use such mechanisms to publicize their available assets**, especially in the private sector—while continuing to make resources available year after year. So it augurs well when your proposal writer/consultant understands this, and digs up potential funding sources without any overt action on their part. Ultimately then, a proposal writer's skills need to be broad enough to open up the nonprofit funding marketplace in all its permutations.

So you, the internal organizational consultant and marketing whiz, will need to emerge from internal deliberations, bring your considerable skills together, and use the written word to present your organization credibly and vigorously. This might take the form of a laboriously constructed government funding application, a simple proposal letter to a private funder, or a face-to-face pitch to an individual. Whatever the situation, your ability to excel and reflect your organization's credibility and qualifications in writing will emerge from that inside detailing work, much of which you made happen.

Convener, communicator, facilitator, researcher, writer— these attributes make it possible to visualize an appropriately dense definition of the craft of those who make resource development their business, sweeping aside the ludicrous concept of the grant writer while also going beyond a singular focus on grants.

A nonprofit executive was heard to intone solemnly in a board meeting that, when it came to going after grants, it was all about the writing. The rejoinder: Going after grants involves much more than writing, and for proposals, the substance of the writing, not the style, matters.

Your organization's commitment to a strength-based approach to resource development will foster an environment marked by the following characteristics:

- *The people around you will better understand the importance of your possibly redefined work, along with making themselves available to you.*

- *These people will possess a stronger grasp of the integration between your organization's existence and the funding proposals chosen to represent its mission-driven efforts, enabling your nonprofit to strongly compete in an ever more crowded funding marketplace.*

- *You will create compelling proposals, useful when presented among a variety of funders and, at the same time, equally potent as a basis for cementing and extending competencies of others in your organization when they participate in their creation.*

Think of it this way: There are many ways to write funding proposals, but no single best way. If, however, you orchestrate and develop proposals to reflect your organization's mission-driven strategy, either in part or whole, the interactive, interpersonal process that finds you doing much more than writing will also contribute to a healthy internal environment and reinforce or even clarify the mission. And you will emerge with a proposal revealing your organization's values along with its intentions.

As internal benefits become apparent to you and the people you've drawn into your work, the exercise of developing proposals evolves from what is sometimes described as drudgery to a stimulating venture into the real workings of your nonprofit.

There is even value to the developmental process, when no funds are forthcoming from the investor you've approached. This is not to suggest an affinity for masochism—no one seeking resources enjoys declinations—but they overwhelm the instances where proposals are funded. There are far more noes than yeses when it comes to seeking financial support from external sources. Framed by that reality, the need to be persistent, to learn what you might from a particular proposal's journey, suggests that today's rejection is tomorrow's success. A former workshop participant epitomized such shrewdness when relating that he had asked for and received the opportunity to sit down with a staff member of the foundation that had declined his organization's initial proposal. Smart cookie, that guy.

Now we move from the craft of nonprofit resource development to frame it within the environment where it unfolds.

CHAPTER FOUR

FINDING A

How to pursue more and better opportunities for your nonprofit

Leverage Your Board.

Yikes! You have a board! Since we are about to dig into the enduring nonprofit business of digging around for resources, we'll start by acknowledging that an organization doing this typically includes a volunteer board of directors. While staff in nonprofits often orchestrate efforts to keep programs going, as well they might, there are those board members in there somewhere. So, this suggests it would be advantageous should these board members add to the strength of a resilient organization—a possibility if your organizational culture finds them willing to take on several key functions. These are:

- *Providing financial oversight and accountability*
- *Broadening perspective about the organization's efforts through sharing their own experiences*
- *Using connections to other individuals and organizations to benefit their nonprofit's work*
- *Financially supporting their own organization as a prerequisite to opening up other sources of potential support*
- *Adding to the credibility of their organization by periodically assuming appropriate leadership*

Such sensible board capacities don't appear to germinate all that easily in nonprofit culture. This suggests why there is something akin to a cottage industry dedicated to imparting the ideal characteristics and functions of nonprofit boards. Nonetheless, for all that is proffered in books, podcasts and trainings, many boards remain problematic, particularly when it comes to playing a part in the quest for resources.

Haven't we all at some time or another been exposed to or been party to sniping about such boards? Heard the deadly homophone where board is spelled bored? Learned of the willingness of board members to do everything except hunker down and raise money? Gossiped about members who operate on the basis of their personalities rather than agreed-upon principles? Sad litany.

So, what to do? Beyond acknowledging this often unfortunate characteristic in the nonprofit realm, all we can add here is that there's plenty of room for members of a nonprofit board to participate in the approach to resource development this book will champion. If those on your board do their part to tangibly support the accomplishment of organizational mission, you might be able to legitimately claim that yours is an extraordinary nonprofit. And, if you think about it, wouldn't you want to weigh in with such an exceptional organization in the brawling arena where resources await the applicants for their use?

We'll get back to nonprofit boards and look at some prospects for down-to-earth support for your nonprofit when we discuss making your efforts real in CHAPTER 6.

Don't Chase — Seek.

Moving on, there was a time some years ago where my responsibility as a program officer in a substantially endowed community foundation included making judgments about the prospects of organizations whose funding proposals were sent our way, and assigned to me. Reviewing each proposal, leading up to a recommendation about funding, almost always included a site visit.

During such a visit, I always got around to asking how the applicant for funding decided to submit the proposal we were discussing; whether it defined an approach to resource development that included staff and board in anything akin to an overall strategy; and whether the implications of the short-term nature of our grantmaking had been considered?

Answers varied from squirming because we were discussing these matters for the first time, to introducing other team members into our meeting to broaden the conversation. While this afforded my counterparts the opportunity to indicate some sense of organizational resource development strategy, the answers often devolved to knowing that the foundation had plenty of money, distributed grants four times a year, so it was worth taking a stab at some funding. The shallowness of such a response was symptomatic of something we at the foundation understood as the "you got it, we need it" syndrome.

One applicant minced no words when responding, reminding me that she knew our foundation had millions in the bank, her tiny nonprofit had none, and when would they get theirs from us, thank you very much.

I had a couple of takeaways after a bunch of these meetings. One was that we had opened up a conversation rarely held otherwise. Another, that the questions and discussions we had opened up might have stimulated the prospect of more thinking, perhaps even action, to firm up resource development strategies within the applicant organization after the visit concluded.

The awkwardness of these experiences—especially the evidence of little forethought about approaching and interacting with a prospective benefactor—is not confined to what happened on these site visits. I got to see the phenomenon in general when proposals came through the door at the foundation, and organizations would appeal for funding on figurative bended knee, the supplicant's stance.

It quickly became apparent that there were folks in such outfits who knew enough to know there were funders out and about, and little else. We came to understand that their proposals were among the many listless pleas for survival scattered all over the place, changing only the destination address every time one was submitted. Known as shotgunning proposals, this unfortunate practice was and is altogether too common, and rests on the notion that just maybe one of the many pitches would bring some money through the doors.

This jaded practice even at times became a topic of conversation among those of us whose organizations had been approached. Phone call with kindred program officer: "Didja get a letter proposal pitch from from..." interrupting, "yeah we got it, and so did everyone else..." You get the point.

There's no such think as a so-called GRANT WRITER

There is you,
however,

For all the damning connotations of such sloppiness, among the most obvious to flare up is when someone reading your proposal easily concludes that it reflects little more than something thrown together by some poor soul in your organization.

This also gives credence to the perception that non-profits often seem riddled with neediness and dwell in desperation—hardly the stuff of presenting yours from a position of strength and resilience in its natural setting, as previously conveyed.

This dreariness also presents itself when digging into the process behind the lousy product, to put it bluntly. It isn't unusual, as previously inferred, to find outfits where even suggesting collective staff time for labor-intensive resource development often loses out to competing interests. Everyone's too busy.

Further, how often is fundraising described as a necessary evil at best by people who revel in the programs they deliver within a nonprofit? This, while all the while failing to understand the connection between being able to do what they do and the importance of maintaining the resources that make this possible.

As short-sighted as such a viewpoint is, it is equally regrettable because it foregoes the opportunity an organization has to use the process of pursuing external resources to also strengthen itself at the same time. (Stay tuned.)

Too, there are those harried souls on staff expected to go after resources, but count fundraising or resource development as the last of their multiple responsibilities. And then, the persistently mislabeled grant writers expected to succeed in solitary splendor because others in the organizational mix are otherwise occupied.

Taken together, the elements of this slapdash approach are a set-up for failure most likely to result in hastily assembled, poorly understood proposals resulting in dreaded funding declinations.

Even at this, there's an off chance of scoring funds through a rash of activity by an occasionally hyperactive grant maker. In spite of the ostensible success, you're likely to be reminded when chasing down that next grant that the money through your door is only as important as the quality of effort it makes possible. To make the point, if your nonprofit doesn't own that ill-funded proposal that led to some money because it was cobbled together by an isolated operative, it will own the effects of the ill-conceived program efforts to follow.

And, as for owning your proposal, to stay with this angle, it's reasonable to visualize this if—and this is a big if—everyone to be involved should it be funded, along with intended beneficiaries, participates in building it. (This is no less important even when your organization has chosen to use the services of a proposal writer for hire.)

Two Resource Development Strategies

- *Being Proactive*
- *Inside-Out*

Let's push away from the trappings of what is so often business as usual when nonprofits chase money. Rather, let's dig into the substance of two tactical alternatives through which to pursue resources. Each points out how your organization could end up with the judicious development and use of a funding proposal. And each embodies the business as unusual that this book champions for your use.

You may very well know something about the first tactic, either practically or theoretically. It is steeped in common sense. The second, steeped in potential, and apt to strike you as an unusual strategy, awaits your courage in embracing my convictions that it will serve your organization well.

Before we get to the details, it's necessary to acknowledge a facet of reality that confronts the inherent or potential creativity of your efforts. The soundness of conceptualizing your organization's mission-driven efforts to span multiple years is indisputable, and will underlie the discussions to follow. BUT. The vagaries of external funding in all their forms might find you settling on a year-to-year approach when it comes to reaching out for financial assistance. This acknowledges that grant makers are renowned for rewarding the gravitas of fabled long-range planning of the five-year variety with one-year grants. There are precious few long-term commitments from the funding side of the nonprofit equation. As for the now burgeoning support alternatives to grants identified previously, their availability seems to be every bit as episodic, thereby also militating against longer-range possibilities.

Strategy 1: Being Proactive

Moving on, let's consider the first of the previously mentioned strategies, and label it Proactivism. It is exemplified when some sharp people in nonprofit organizations, mindful of the rarely ending quest for operating resources, make it their business to doggedly poke around for and react to funding possibilities wherever they manage to dig them up.

These are the staff members—or perhaps consultants—who would use a tool such as the *NONPROFIT ENGINE ON PAGE 10* as a guide to dig into the opportunities for resource development displayed.

They take on the responsibility to know, for example, that Google is filled with information that invites searches galore. They're the ones who consult Notices of Funding Availability in the Federal Register; or show up at a bidder's conference conducted by a high profile, active grant maker; or scour the web persistently to poke around in topical sites such as WWW.GRANTS.GOV for federal funding possibilities, that in turn might lead to State Agency funding possibilities; as well as local government funding passed through to nonprofit organizations.

Or they make it their business to consult The Foundation Center's website, WWW.FOUNDATIONCENTER.ORG, for data about private sector giving, or participate as members in a topically apt listserv of kindred resource seekers.

Not only this, but these are the people who would also make it their business to bedevil board members about taking responsibility for helping to design fundraising events, as well as occasionally sitting down face to face to ask individual donors to stand and deliver.

And they're likely to be the ones who go so far as to dig around for funding opportunities not so readily apparent. For example, reaching out and contacting organizations that have already been funded—learned through word of mouth, press release, grantee lists—to ask for guidance about how to approach any organization that has supported them.

Two essential points: Those carrying out such intentional, enterprising tactics for pursuing resources value and respect a dynamic, healthy organizational environment, a powerful credible connotation; and these folks fully embrace a conscious set of tactics aimed at finding and engaging the other half of the nonprofit equation, the funders and investors out there.

What should be clear is that, among all things nonprofit, these practices and the attitude behind them reflect awareness that we need to shoulder the responsibility to continuously identify and seek out prospective resources to support our mission-driven efforts.

Strategy 2: Inside-Out

The second strategy in pursuing resources, Inside-Out,

is, frankly, a best practice in waiting, but damn it, it is a best practice! So, open your mind's eye and come along as we visualize, then, a creative approach to organizational behavior that strikes me as would be useful, without exception, among nonprofits.

This would find members and allies of a nonprofit gathered together—sensibly assisted by someone to facilitate the process—to review past and present efforts to carry out its mission-driven work, and then to contemplate what would remain to be done to actually accomplish that mission.

Further, these folks in and close to the nonprofit organization would also take the time to contribute to decisions about why, when and where to seek out prospective resources to support their organization's labors—especially with the guidance of a sharp resource-developer type in the mix .

An exceptional, collective strength-based definition of pursuing resources would emerge as part of the organization's broader, agreed upon operating strategy. This would constitute a creative alternative to the practice of generic organizational development based on long-range planning, and much bandied about in the nonprofit sector as something akin to a cottage industry.

So, we would supplant conventional context, and embrace Inside-Out, our best practice in-the-making, depicting thoughtful, reflective and predictive communication among those gathered together to agree on collective efforts looking toward the future.

Imagine, then, that these deliberations would lead you and yours—gathered to, in effect, look out the window and down the road in the direction of the future—to visualize and agree on how far your organization should continue traveling in pursuit of its mission always bearing in mind that the destination at the end of the road traveled is the mission accomplished.

You'd also need to estimate a chunk of travel time to continue your outfit's intended efforts to help participants make progress in improving the quality of their lives. Set aside the previously cited funders' one-year stricture as this is a concerted effort at creativity and, on your own terms, design a manageable longer term segment in the proposed journey. Arbitrarily, two to three years has a nice ring to it...

And, once your deliberations lead to clarity about what you propose to undertake during this next phase, you'd need to assess the cost to pay the fare for this leg of the trip to progress, so to say, as well as eventually determining where to pursue resources. In other words, the importance of needed resources comes back into focus, and some financial and funding source forecasting is in the works.

The take-away from your deliberations will almost inevitably be confirmation that your organization does not have all the money it needs to pay for the trip, as we're calling it. The phenomenon of the under-resourced non-profit is not unusual, and persistently informs the process of seeking external funds.

So when sensibly approaching relatively over-resourced organizations, the funders that is, you want to do so in a persuasive way. (To repeat, this will be enhanced by the quality of previous deliberations that bring you to verify among yourselves where your organization is in terms of its accomplishments, what remains to be done in pursuit of its mission, what resources you bring to your efforts, and what resources should be sought. This, in turn, sets up the basis by which you are able to offer a powerful argument for pursuing grants or any other external funding mechanism.)

With this in mind, take a look at the following two scenarios for moving beyond your deliberations into action. In each, the mark of an unusually strong organization emerges because your proposal describes what amounts to a partnership between equals in an arena marked by the inequality between the funders and the occasionally funded.

Think about it. Such a proposition offers a prospective benefactor the opportunity to back a winner, a desirable, notable departure from the run-of-the-mill applicant-as-supplicant previously mentioned.

In the first setting, it is essential that your proposal makes clear that funding is sought to help underwrite the costs of the fully described next phase in your organization's mission-based labors to bring about community change. This, and equally important, to clarify that your organization is bringing its own resources into the proposed mix of activities. These assets, often in-kind, are presented as an inducement to generate the requested

WHEREVER

YOU TELL IT.

Highlight where your organization is in terms of its accomplishments, what remains to be done in pursuit of its mission, what resources you bring to your efforts, and what resources should be sought.

external resources that, in turn, fill in the gaps to fully finance your proposed effort.

As straightforward as looking to fill gaps is, here's a second, rarely articulated, strength-based resource-seeking theme that can spill out of the willingness to communicate internally before soliciting assistance. Picture a situation where your deliberations confirm that the combination of resources your organization has at its disposal would allow it to continue with most aspects of program delivery for the coming year. You have, let's say, some carryover funding available from a previous grant, the net proceeds from several community-based fundraising events, just secured a modest fee-for-service contract, and a substantial array of contributed resources (facilities, furnishings, volunteers). These combined assets would allow your organization to continue its mission-driven work.

This conjures the vivid image of yours as one of the more effective nonprofits because it constantly stitches together the assets to keep plugging away, all things considered, a good thing. At the same time, this might lead to the conclusion that searching for additional resources is out of the question, albeit because of your enterprising nature. Not necessarily.

Suppose, when deliberating as we've defined it here, you and yours, with a lot of impetus from your talented proposal writer/resource developer/consultant, imagine moving beyond your organization's current measure of resource sufficiency. This leads you to conceive of increasing the scope of your work, while also agreeing this would fit the ever-present focus on making progress to complete your organization's mission. In this case, bigger is better.

Where before we discussed seeking resources to fill gaps, this strategy for seeking additional resources is based on adding value to your efforts by thoughtfully and sensibly proposing to expand them. And so your excellent proposal would reflect this. And, your tactics might continue on such a basis for as long as needed and as long as it made sense.

We'll continue with this creative business as unusual for going after resources in *CHAPTER 6*. But first, if you want to come to the place where robust resource development asserts itself as a mark of how your organization operates, we have more ground to cover.

WHEN IT COMES TO FUNDING...

OR

CHAPTER FOUR

TAKEAWAYS

Leverage Your Board.

Their connections, contributions and participation can go a long way.

Don't Chase—Seek.

Instead of spending time and effort going after ill-fitting grants, pursue resources in a more thoughtful way that aligns with your organization's mission.

Two Resource Development Strategies

The approach you take will be a measure of your organization's creativity and vitality. Either will benefit from your New Proposal Framework *(OUTLINED IN CHAPTERS 5 AND 6).*

1. Being Proactive

Much better than being reactive and waggable, this approach takes advantage of opportunities to fuel the Nonprofit Engine. *(SEE GRAPHIC ON PAGE 10.)*

2. Inside-Out

The ideal way to secure funds that any mission-driven nonprofit should strive toward, this approach calls for an examination of why the nonprofit exists (people's needs), what should be accomplished (impact), and how it would realistically operate over time (logistics).

CHAPTER FIVE

YOUR NEW

Rebuilding the elements of a funding proposal in a more compelling and logical structure

There are assorted formats for developing proposals scattered around the nonprofit sector, including those required by some prospective funders. Ranging from elaborate to unadorned,they always present the challenge of how to organize them, although common sense suggests you follow directions in any event.

But then, governed by the strength-based approach to resource development unfolding here, equal common sense leads to using the singular format for developing proposals that follows, no matter their intended destination. Because this/our framework emphasizes the muscle of the case for needed change on which other elements of your proposal depend for their credibility, its use is always to your advantage in an arena often marked by needy pleading. And, you can manage the challenge of adapting what you've developed this way to a funder's required layout.

Your New Proposal Framework:

- *Begins with a synopsis of what follows— the* SUMMARY

- *Goes on to describe the organization seeking resources and the qualities that distinguish it, in a section labeled* INTRODUCTION TO THE APPLICANT FOR FUNDING

- *Documents concerns about the challenges confronting the people for whom the applicant organization exists, the ones at the heart of the organization's mission in a segment termed the* CASE FOR NEEDED CHANGE

- *Describes the proposed resolution of those challenges in the section* **DEFINING PARTICIPANT SUCCESS**

- *Indicates how the applicant will work, and with whom, to bring about such resolution and success by describing* **PROGRAM STRATEGY**

- *Defines how, as a funded or resourced entity, the applicant will be transparent and accountable for its efforts to bring about change by detailing* **EVALUATION METHODS**

- *Itemizes assets to be combined with funds requested to successfully execute the proposed program described as* **BLENDING RESOURCES**

- *Presents plans for future support, if the program is to continue beyond the period for which funding is sought, in* **MAINTAINING CONTINUITY**

- *And finally, itemizes how much the proposed efforts, in the form of the program strategy and evaluation methods, will cost, including the amount requested from the prospective funder/ investor in the* **BUDGET AND BUDGET NARRATIVE**

Take comfort in realizing that this framework is likely to contain the elements you will find in just about any funding format you encounter, although not necessarily in the order presented. (Two familiar grantmaking foundations most recently re-encountered use an application format largely consistent with this one.)

START SEEING THE

OF EACH PROPOSAL.

Look at every proposal as an opportunity to strengthen how your organization realizes its meaningful, well-defined mission.

The bad news in any quest for commonality is that there are those structured (per)versions, something akin to a pleading form letter, filled with lifeless, repetitive words, where the only change is the destination address. We've all seen these beauties.

The good news in this quest is that, when using a set of reasonable principles to reflect your organization's thinking, all related to the persistent pursuit of a vital mission, the idea of what is often labeled a boilerplate proposal has merit. The funding proposal built initially using the process described in the next chapter will prove useful **every** time you develop a proposal thereafter. The substance of your proposal will stand out.

This moves us to a critical but potent departure in common practice when writing a funding proposal. It takes the form of a distinctive tactic to emphasize what is most important within any such document. When building your proposal, divide the presentation format into two segments rather than simply following it.

And rather than emphasizing the program for which we seek funds, we begin by making the case for mounting such an effort in the first place. This is essential because, to repeat, there is a mania for projects or process rather than outcomes or impact among nonprofits. The net effect is akin to inundating improved quality of life among people for whom a nonprofit exists in an ocean of activities.

The allure of the project presents itself time and again. Example: A college teacher sought funds to augment her performance in the classroom with new technology applications. When asked how she would make the case for her request, she emphasized the intrigue of embracing new teaching techniques. There was no mention of improved student performance, nor students beneficially using what was learned in the classroom outside the classroom to justify the expense for learning newness. True story.

What's wrong with this? Seems like business as usual and that's what's wrong—business as usual. It's as if these narrowly defined projects, so predominant as the basis for seeking resources, take on a life of their own. Familiarity and comfort with a project mentality overwhelm two far more important considerations when developing proposals—the ability to justify any project by discussing why it is needed in the first place, and then clarifying the intended benefits for the people involved in the project after it is completed.

This is why we'll shift the order in the presentation format to develop these most important elements first, before returning them to their original order for submission. This is another form of business as unusual, encapsulated in the following schematic.

This schematic depicts and reinforces unpacking or pulling apart the presentation format into a rearranged proposal building sequence, marked by two phases that will influence your work as the person orchestrating the production of a proposal in your organization. Recall the needed skills to accompany the work of each phase—first your ability to be an internal consultant, then a marketing specialist.

YOUR NEW PROPOSAL FRAMEWORK

DEVELOPMENT

Build in this order to emphasize first things first.

PHASE ONE

- CASE FOR NEEDED CHANGE
- DEFINING PARTICIPANT SUCCESS
- PROPOSED PROGRAM STRATEGY
- EVALUATION METHODS

PHASE TWO

- APPLICANT FOR FUNDING
- BLENDING RESOURCES
- MAINTAINING CONTINUITY
- BUDGET AND BUDGET NARRATIVE
- SUMMARY

FINALIZATION

Reorganize for a clear and potent presentation.

- SUMMARY
- APPLICANT FOR FUNDING
- CASE FOR NEEDED CHANGE
- DEFINING PARTICIPANT SUCCESS
- PROPOSED PROGRAM STRATEGY
- EVALUATION METHODS
- BLENDING RESOURCES
- MAINTAINING CONTINUITY
- BUDGET AND BUDGET NARRATIVE

The first proposal construction phase is critically important because the four elements you will tackle— Case for Needed Change, Defining Participant Success, Proposed Program Strategy, and Evaluation Methods, form the core of your proposal in that order. This is where you can undo project mania by beginning your work at a different beginning, and first focusing on the need for change that will be the basis for justifying your proposal in its entirety.

The second phase of your New Proposal Framework is dedicated to bringing forward and describing the applicant for funding consideration. This is done by creatively building the Introduction to the Applicant, then discussing Blending Resources, Maintaining Continuity, and finally detailing the Budget and documenting it in the related Budget Narrative. Your focus should lead to presenting prospective funders with the features of an enterprising organization to deliver the program presented in the first-developed core of your proposal.

Once the two-phase proposal construction process has been completed, you will reorganize what has been created back into the original presentation format (as mentioned in our initial discussion) and meld the Summary into it.

This leads us to the opportunity to bring these elements to life so they comprise the essence of a persuasive funding proposal. We do this by working through the components of your New Proposal Framework, the discussion of which follows—no small matter as you'll see. This is because the present and proposed makeup of your own nonprofit, along with associated activities, must be assessed before it is possible to arrive at your strategic intentions going forward. If you grasp the imparted wisdom of strengthening your nonprofit while building its funding proposal, you'll come to value that there is a whole lot more to creating that document than writing.

CHAPTER SIX

BRINGING IT

How to build out the New Proposal Framework, section by section

This is where we will visualize how your in-house proposal writer, or consultant, interacts with those to be involved in developing a funding proposal. This means examining what it will take to build each element in the two-phase proposal construction process just illustrated, emerging with a solid final product.

What follows, however, is anything but bandying about how to use proposal development terminology to guide how to create your document. We will replace what often passes for conventional wisdom and proposal-speak with concepts intended to stimulate creative thinking, influence internal communication, and crystallize your resultant findings as markers of your organization's continued progress as an effective nonprofit.

Case for Needed Change

Begin with the basis for any funding proposal, the Case for Needed Change. There's a lot to chew on here. This is the section of a proposal that is often labeled, Problem Statement or Assessment of Needs. Resist using either term because each reinforces the worst aspects of how we relate to the environment in which our organizations operate.

Let's start with notion of need. This term is so common in proposals it's as if it were a commodity being offered at greater and greater levels among members of a so-called target group as a basis for justifying requests. It seems a hideous contradiction that an organization whose reason for existence is based on preserving the dignity and well-being of the people it works with, would reduce them to objects of neediness. The term is also used repeatedly to claim that people need programs for which funding is sought, a classic unsupported assumption given the usual absence of any qualifying data. As a practical and ethical matter, we need to do away with the concept.

The use of the term, problem, for this aspect of your proposal development proves, well, problematic. This is exemplified when so many proposals express that there is a problem because there are people in a community who have not as yet been involved in the program proposed for funding. This makes it easy to ask the proper and debilitating question, So what? There may be reasons to suggest value for people to participate in a proposed program, but not before explaining why in terms that describe their circumstances, and have nothing to do with your proposed program. Yet.

Here's a real life example of doing away with the problem statement approach to proposal building. An educator developing a proposal to bring technology into the classroom to augment his teaching methods struggled with using the term Problem Statement. When asked why, he responded that, while the absence of optimal student learning was his concern, he found the apparent requirement to describe students as problem-laden unacceptable because it mischaracterized them with a negative label.

He ended up deleting the ostensible conventional approach, and substituted the descriptor, Unrealized Opportunities for Classroom Learners. This became the basis for the proposal (the case for needed change, as we're defining it here and now). The missing optimal learning was later specified in the proposal as measurably improved student performance (see defining participant success, details to follow) made possible by describing the use of technology to produce such change for the better (describing program strategy, also to follow).

Let's broaden the implications of this example of creativity in working through a funding proposal. Just as the educator did, you might possibly argue that you're pursuing funds to foster needed change in the way your organization works with people. This would be impressive if you base such an argument on what was learned from an evaluation of your previous efforts, and prove intriguing as the basis for a proposal to retool your tactics, in effect proposing a new project rather than seeking continuation funding for the original. In a project-intensive funding arena rife with requests from nonprofits to just keep going, this seems like a sharp tactic.

Back to the immediate business at hand. Since you have been admonished to supplant conventional terminology in making the case for funding, where does this leave you in clarifying how to make that case? You can see by the educator's example that there are different, creative angles to describe the basis for change. This ingenuity is refreshing and long overdue—as long as you never deviate from focusing this section of your funding proposal on the (likely compromised) quality of the lives of people for whom your organization exists—let's call them your folks—the ones who form the basis for its mission.

Let's take this discussion further by envisioning your organization's soundness, hopefully not the unsupported kind that often renders proposals suspect. It seems reasonable, then, to assume that yours is a mission-driven nonprofit organization helping people improve the quality of their lives, something you choose to describe in more specific terms in a funding proposal.

If so, then your internal deliberations when developing such a document will find you beginning at the beginning, so to say. This means you and yours will work to verify and describe the human circumstances among your folks that call for change, nothing more, nothing less.

You might label these as barriers or challenges or, as we just saw, unrealized opportunities. The point is that the persistent tendency in so many proposals to make a project the primary object of attention is discarded in favor of authenticating conditions that will lead to the wisdom of mounting any such project.

Continuing to discuss how you discovered such conditions requiring change may well afford you the opportunity to relate in your proposal that what you've learned flows from day-to-day connections within a community, or with group members or perhaps previous program participants. This reflects well on your organization because it confirms the respect shown for the perspectives of those you intend to support to improve the quality of their lives.

You might also have the benefit of using research-based data to corroborate and add weight to the challenges discovered among your prospective recipients. In this era of comprehensive information technology, a massive store of data is only a computer click away.

You also might benefit from looking around, as well, for the work of general purpose planning organizations, perhaps engaged in demographic research, along with graduate department researchers in higher education to see if you can glean relevant data to support your own findings.

You'll also need to specify the number of people targeted to benefit from your efforts yet to be described. You may draw conclusions about this using something as stark as triage, where comparative urgency will require imposing limits on the number of people assisted. Or the circumstances among your prospective participants may be far more benign, as might be hoped, but you will nonetheless need to arrive at a population count. This acknowledges limits on the level of effort your organization can realistically shoulder. And, you may find there are limitations from and among external funding prospects as to scale of effort they will support.

Another aspect of uncovering a situation that troubles your target group entails understanding factors that contribute to its existence and, therefore, the implications for what you will propose to overcome them. Next, a hypothetical to illustrate.

Suppose the staff of your community center has become aware of and shares a concern with a group of area people about their not being gainfully employed, with the associated benefits. You've come to learn this because those afflicted regularly participate in a variety of center activities, and make it their business to let your staff know about the vicissitudes of their daily lives. Everyone agrees that this situation has to change for the better—these people want jobs—and the center's broadly defined mission is to assist them to improve the quality of their lives.

In beginning to formulate a strategy to promote employment, staff will need to assess what factors contribute to the current unemployment. Perhaps those without work have not learned the skills required to apply for or hold onto a job; or unemployment persists because there are no accessible jobs to be had. Maybe both factors lead to this unwelcome, unacceptable stasis. The ability to clearly assess and understand the facets of this situation in need of change would obviously dictate strategy and tactics included should a proposal to promote employment emerge.

Perhaps you'd also be dealing with a situation that has earlier evoked concern, a challenge that persists in spite of previous attempts to overcome it. You might think of this as unfinished business. Your tactics to continue dealing with such a situation might vary from building on past, partial success to safeguarding against repeating previous ineffectiveness.

The point is, however it unfolds, a clearly articulated and documented situation in need of change provides the substance of this section of your proposal. It also forms the basis for what follows when you define such change in terms that represent participant success, and then describe the strategy you propose to bring about change and achieve success.

The line of thoughtful reasoning by which you are being asked to conceptualize proposal development, beginning with the substance of what was just presented, is every bit as important as evidence of organizational values as it is the basis for a powerful plan-in-the-making. If your outfit operates with an unwavering commitment to help people improve the quality of their lives, this strongly communicates justification for its continued existence.

If you have no such mission-based clarity, or have somehow lost it, and have managed one way or another to get some dollars through the door, it would be difficult to refute a harsh observation that your organization writes proposals to chase after money to keep some staff employed and run programs at people.

There's another facet of organizational values that fits here in this discussion of proposal development. Since our proposals begin by focusing on the circumstances that diminish the quality of the lives of the people most important to our organization, those very people must agree with what this says about them. If this is not evident, it would be reasonable to question the soundness of the foundational argument for needed change.

Bear in mind, as well, that there may be divergence in the outlook and experiences of staff in nonprofits and the participants to be involved when it comes to formulating programs for which funds will be sought. So, the authenticity of what materializes in our proposals is much less susceptible to dispute if provisions are made to acknowledge participant perspective. One way of accomplishing this is by substantively involving the intended beneficiaries of proposed programs in the planning of such efforts and, for that matter, in the day-to-day organizational operations.

Support

solutions

the people

you serve.

Think of this as running programs with the folks for whom our organization exists rather than running programs at them.

Before continuing with the construction process, let's stay with the substance of organizational values, and again consider the internal give and take advocated here for pulling together a funding proposal. Given this, your organization might choose to employ a consultant to work on crafting your funding proposals. The wisdom of such a move would depend on a simple but critical distinction about how your outside expert works inside. If your consultant writes proposals for an organization, it's a thanks-but-no-thanks situation. If the consultant builds proposals with an organization, your outfit's values will shine through to imprint that person's labors.

We now move from documenting the need for change among those we might describe as target group members to the only concept that would legitimately follow, describing such change in detail. Once again, we will supplant conventional wisdom that recommends the use of the terms, Outcomes or Objectives. And just as previous traditional terminology gave way to our developing a far more vital concept, the same happens here and now where we label needed change as Defining Participant Success.

Defining Participant Success

Defining Participant Success takes into consideration how often the terms, Outcomes or Objectives, are used erroneously in funding proposals. This is typified by the following from one such proposal stating that its objective is to educate 500 participants about healthcare access, by developing and delivering healthcare access orientation sessions.

Though not made clearly evident in the subject proposal, one could infer—though should not need to—that the challenge driving this activity-as-objective is that people were having difficulty accessing healthcare. If so, the only justifiable objective or outcome, or better yet, definition of participant success, is to describe that those people will benefit by gaining access to previously missing healthcare.

The misidentified item, education, exemplifies the temptation to get ahead of ourselves by jumping into describing our best efforts to work with participants in programs we intend to implement. There's no room for this here, because this section of your funding proposal in effect belongs to your folks, and discussing what your organization intends to do with them detracts from the proper focus on their well-being. Were we to recast the subject proposal, we would define participant success by stating that 500 participants would benefit from gaining access to previously unavailable healthcare in a precise time frame—as a result of orientation and education to be further explained in the section on program tactics to follow.

Remember, our proposal development begins by describing predicaments faced by our folks, so it follows that we next define eliminating these in language that reflects successful participant behavior. Doesn't it make enduring sense to clearly understand and describe the ultimate

Remember,

(not projects).

impact of the program you will propose before describing the program itself? After all, such a program is unquestionably justified when designed to foster needed change that culminates in thriving participants.

Defining Participant Success should be marked by precise measures. This means that successful behavior described here is exact enough to be measured when mounting the evaluation later described in your proposal. Further, specifying the number of people reported as attaining success, likely members of what you'll define as a target group, will set up the subsequent discussion of the scope of your intended program.

This will also make it possible for a prospective funder/investor to judge your detailed program strategy on the basis of a true cost-benefit analysis. This means ultimately assessing your effort not only as to how much the program you are about to describe will deliver for the money requested in the budget, but even more important, the level of associated participant benefits at such a cost.

If your target group is to embrace the definition of its success, what you propose must be meaningful. Here's an example to make the point. A member of a team developing a community-based proposal enthusiastically shared that one definition of success for the participants would be their ability to keep journals, something they had never previously done. Setting aside whether producing journals was an end in itself, or whether there were other benefits as a result of journal-keeping that might more properly illustrate success, the proposed outcome was a prescription for failure because it did not take into account that demographic data used to characterize the community of would-be writers included evidence of a high level of illiteracy.

We also need to remember to modify success indicators to conform with time constraints of impermanent funding sources, most of which, as you know, make resources available on a short-term basis. This is very likely to lead to defining participant success in incremental stages or phases. Another reason to pay attention to this is because you do not want to compromise organizational credibility by over-promising success that cannot be reasonably and timely attained.

To wrap up this aspect of an unfolding developmental process, your ability and willingness to present specific definitions of participant success strengthen your proposal and, once again, reflect well on your organization. This translates into moving beyond what we earlier characterized as unfortunately all too common among nonprofits—the comfort from being busy. In this time when so many organizations vie for attention and funding, you will distinguish yours by presenting it as one willing to be judged on much more than being busy—being effective.

Proposed Program Strategy

The third of this initial four-part phase in proposal development is Proposed Program Strategy. Whereas business as usual might refer to this as Program Implementation, we emphasize the concept of strategy as another indicator of the dynamism of our proposal-in-the-making.

Being strategic includes making certain that you explain why you believe the approach you are choosing will prove effective before delving into it. Are you, for example, mounting another version of a program your organization has successfully carried out before? Or are you emulating a project that has been successful elsewhere, something akin to a model project? Perhaps your values include what might be called a theory of change by which your mission-driven work is pursued, with the proposed effort accordingly representative. Best of all, how about communicating your conviction that the proposed effort will be effective because the people expected to benefit from its completion helped to build it.

Here's an example where failing to consider such an approach torpedoed a proposal. On a site visit to discuss a proposal for organizing urban neighborhood street youth, representatives of the applicant nonprofit were asked why they were confident that their project would work. They responded that they planned to enlist participation of known leaders among the targeted youth, as well as securing endorsement of the project and participation from local law enforcement. They had approached neither, and could in no way verify their willingness to be involved. So two unsupported assumptions zapped the credibility of their request.

Once all who should be part of the development process agree about program substance, you'll also want to agree on a sequence of events to fit the constrained time frame typically accompanying external funding commitments.

This is likely to lead to a linear display of activities or tasks across the span of a year.

Or perhaps, as previously envisioned, your group took the time to figuratively look out your nonprofit window, so you will be ambitious enough to spread such activities over more than one year even though you are not likely to find opportunities for multi-year support. The point in considering this longer range is that it distinguishes your organization by virtue of articulating the continuation of its efforts beyond the period for which it seeks funds.

You'll also need to specify staff, materials and facilities to comprise the span of your proposed effort. Make sure, as well, to explain how you intend to oversee the proposed project, something suggesting the work of skilled management staff, and its inclusion in your budget allocations. This oversight function, always important, is even more demanding if the description of your efforts includes mutually agreeable collaboration with one or more organizations, so much so, that another aspect of your proposed collaboration is likely to include details in a memo of understanding as part of the proposed strategy.

Take into account that each project activity you delineate must contribute to accomplishing previously described participant success. To reinforce this prime connection—rather than attempting to define project activities from start to finish, use each outcome defining participant success as the starting point from which to develop your program tactics. Do this by working your way back to project start up, defining the train of activities undertaken to culminate in participant success. This validates the credibility-inducing strategy of only building programmatic tactics that make sense and lead to resultant impact.

Evaluation Methods

Time now to focus attention on development of Evaluation Methods, the final element of the core four. Bear in mind that this adds credibility to your proposal by verifying your organization's willingness to be accountable for both the quality of work it intends to carry out and the resultant impact for which it has assumed responsibility.

This is a big deal because it holds out the prospect of substance rather than what passes for evaluation so often in the form of little more than a head count injected into a proposal as a hastily thrown together afterthought. Here are some suggestions for developing down-to-earth tactics to improve on such a dreary situation.

Begin framing your approach to evaluation by understanding that it is part of effective program management. Carrying out your efforts without evaluating them is a form of organizational self indulgence that belies any concern for quality. The consequence of such laziness robs you of the ability to use documented program excellence as the most legitimate inducement to not only continue the quest for external funds, but do it from a position of strength.

Picture evaluation methodology as a sensible set of parallel activities unfolding side by side with the events that evolve when getting your program work underway. And, remember that building and implementing substance in what and how you propose to evaluate won't take place without some labor intensive efforts. This makes it immediately apparent that there is room for including the costs of the dedicated staff and/or consultants among the line items in your proposed budget.

Your proposed approach to this work begins by understanding the need to answer the fundamental evaluation question, *what do we need to learn?* You'll apply that question to both the measures defining participant success and your program strategy, each of which is to be evaluated. This, in turn, will lead to more specific questions.

The more specific evaluation question upon which to design the assessment of your program strategy—you might call this process evaluation or program monitoring—asks if what you set out to accomplish is functioning as intended. The need to discover this becomes apparent as our best laid tactics encounter reality once we get them up and running. This can lead to confronting unforeseen circumstances often characterized as unanticipated variables. This can necessitate the obligation to change what was originally proposed. Example: unforeseen fuel cost increases halfway through a grant-funded rural transportation program that led to retrenching the scope of the originally proposed effort.

There's no mystery in designing a monitoring program to be explained in your proposal. It should be created to facilitate communication among people associated with the proposed project, including its presumed beneficiaries. This will require those people periodically taking time away from other pursuits to review the process underway and to draw conclusions about whether any modifications to the project are in order. What you include in the proposal should express when and how often you intend to meet, and who will be involved. This is the essence of the easier part of completing an evaluation.

As for the more complex aspect of evaluation methodology, we come to the need to design techniques for answering the more specific question, *are participants achieving the success our proposal has stated they would?* This is likely to call for design help from those familiar with creating outcome evaluations, along with what is referred to as the instruments used to deliver them—including pre- and post-intervention interviews or tests, survey questionnaires, and developing and using protocols to conduct focus groups, to name a few.

Perhaps this will find you forging relationships with consultants who earn a living by designing and conducting evaluations. Remembering the recent advice to include evaluation costs in your proposed budget, you may discover that they are willing to help you design an impact evaluation when there is the prospect that your funded proposal will lead to their retention as paid practitioners.

And, if your part of the world includes accessible higher education, digging around might lead you to discover faculty-tended graduate students eager to augment classroom work with the opportunity for service learning. There is a premium to steeping students' experiences with real-life opportunities for learning among people in communities where our nonprofits are active. So perhaps you can orchestrate a win-win scenario in the form of a mutually agreeable evaluation design.

When describing your proposed evaluation, don't neglect to address as best you can how you intend to analyze your findings, mindful that resultant program refinements or retooling epitomize its practical value, and possibly a fundable next phase.

Take the time to include a plan for disseminating your evaluation findings. While the first beneficiaries of what evaluation divulges are the people closest to the assessed program, there is much to support the wisdom of spreading the word about what your organization has come to learn about its good work and the benefits associated with this. If evaluation confirms the significance of your organization's efforts, even in the most subjective terms, wouldn't you want to broadcast this to your current sources of financial support, at a minimum? After celebrating among yourselves...

Finally, take into consideration that proposing to rigorously evaluate your organization's intended efforts presents a solid inducement for financial support by reassuring your prospective funding source of your intention to protect its investment.

Once the proposal development crew under your direction has completed the considerable communication, engagement and labor that culminates in agreement on the definition and explanation of the four elements comprising the core of a funding proposal, you will want to lean into the remaining elements extracted from the presentation format to produce what is required for completion.

You'll do this by shifting your attention to pointing up and verifying the capability of your credible, enterprising organization to deliver the just described core elements of your proposal. Label this Applicant for Funding.

Applicant for Funding

To begin, it seems advisable to carefully consider characteristics that would serve to distinguish your organization since you want proposal readers to visualize your outfit's strengths, no easy matter using the written word alone—and an argument for promoting a site visit from a prospective investor.

In this regard, it's true that your ability to present evidence of credibility is enhanced when you can look back at a detailed track record, as we will discuss further. If not possible, and yours is a relatively new nonprofit, there isn't much in the rear view mirror. Instead, your proposal is confined to highlighting the skills and experience of your founding members, or verifying the emergence of the situation you are proposing to tackle, particularly the legitimacy and urgency of the challenges facing your community members. You also may be creative enough to borrow credibility from other organizations, credible in their own right, that can be persuaded to endorse your efforts. The same may be tried with eminent practitioners in your proposed field of endeavor willing to confirm the importance of what your proposal articulates. (See letters of endorsement, to follow.)

When your organization as an applicant has some history behind it, look for ways to set it apart in a crowded field of competitors for financial support. This leaves all kinds of possibilities, but the following features are offered as food for thought.

First, there is the wisdom of being able to generate evidence of community support, as when people speak out about the value of your organization's ongoing work. This would seem a reasonable by-product when your staff and volunteers consistently interact with community members and program participants so that they freely share their experiences. Or perhaps you've designed and used surveys as part of your evaluation that confirm the high regard participants have for your work with them.

It makes good sense to continuously take snapshots that, in effect, profile the substance of your commitment to help people help themselves. This makes it possible to take what you've captured into a broader public domain.

In this regard, have those in your organization ever considered the prospect of enhancing its integrity by actively pursuing a respectable public relations program as part of your evaluation strategy? Not customary, but remember you're looking for ways to differentiate your outfit. Maybe there's a savvy funder out there who would put some resources in your lap to design such an effort.

Many nonprofits appear to believe that the ability to count heads in their programs represents a measure of quality, especially if there are more heads this year than last. This seems short-sighted. Would it not be far more impressive to indicate who has benefitted and how, among the heads that have been counted? Documenting that your organization is effective along with being busy will go much further to enhance its credibility. This circles back to the importance of evaluation that makes such documentation possible.

Let's return to your volunteer board of directors or trustees. As previously implied, bringing up a nonprofit board sets eyes to rolling, because boards are often anything but an organizational asset. We need not revisit their sins of omission and commission. Rather, it seems sensible to make room for creativity when looking for ways to marshal board resources, and you'd better believe that this is above and beyond showing up for monthly meetings.

How about, for example, imagining that your board was comprised of some members who could—get ready—form a speaker's bureau to represent your organization on the service organization banquet belt.

Or being able to verify that yours is a 100% giving board, meaning that each member regularly contributes cash or in-kind services in lieu of cash. And meaning that there is a marrow conviction within your organization about the hollowness of asking others to support your efforts if your own board won't.

If your board of directors embraces such an enterprising nature, you have a rare organizational asset, and wouldn't want to be bashful about reflecting this every time you try to impress a prospective funding source.

Letters of endorsement are well-known as a means of trying to convince people of your bona fides. Maybe, but only by avoiding misuse, as when fifteen letters are attached to a proposal, each with a different letterhead but precisely the same wording to form a rah-rah cheerleading song, the refrain of which is, fund these folks!

Being inventive enough to seek out letters from people who share distinct knowledge of your organization and its programs—participants, colleagues, experts in your field of work, perhaps even non-hack politicians come to mind—is a far more authentic and impressive version of putting endorsement into play.

Let's revisit the phenomenon of collaboration, a potential mark of distinction for your nonprofit, so often made evident by its absence. This is never more apparent than when prospective funders learn, while reviewing proposals, that there is a crowd of organizations after their money, organizations that appear never to communicate with one another as they clatter around to offer up fragmented, duplicative programs to, in effect, compete with one another.

If, in spite of such a melee, your history documents instances of teaming up to increase program capacity or participant success, any proposal you present that describes another instance of doing this offers up a true point of departure by which to judge its quality.

We cannot discuss organizational excellence without contemplating fiscal soundness. If for no other reason, this is important because your proposal includes a budget, the dollars of which you would have entrusted by benefactors to your outfit's attention and use.

This is another area to legitimize board support, as when you seek to populate it with those wise in the ways of handling money. Think bankers, financial planners, attorneys—remembering that the primary requisite, before any expertise they bring, is their full support of your participant-centered mission.

Sometimes this will find you undertaking or having completed an organizational and program audit, to share the findings with your funder, among others—a requirement that can prove daunting when your organization is expected to finance it. For that matter, maybe the basis for a solid capacity building proposal would find you approaching an external funder to provide the money to underwrite the costs of an initial audit, if your general fund can't support the outlay. Such an investment would broaden your organization's appeal by strengthening its ability to pass fiscal muster when approaching other prospects.

Attesting to fiscal soundness on a less impressive basis can provide you the opportunity for some creativity. It helps, for example, if you have taken advantage of the code among certified public accountants to provide pro bono financial oversight to nonprofits, and have one doing so for your organization.

Finally, if no other facet of maintaining fiscal integrity seems possible, we are left to imagine the importance of having resources to underwrite the cost of the often harried bookkeeper. The presence and labors of such a soul should safeguard your nonprofit from the specter of undocumented expenditures, while also conveying the will-

As often as reasonable, send your carefully crafted proposals, and do so with the conviction that you've clearly shown that your mission deserves funding.

ingness to be transparent. There are no financial secrets in a credible nonprofit organization.

The ideas presented here are but a few, and are intended to inspire you to devise many other angles to portray organizational excellence. When deciding what to include, be aware that credibility is in the eyes of the beholder. With this in mind, look for idiosyncrasies in what potential benefactors seem to value, and even consider attuning the introduction of your organization to account for these. Common ground with a funder is desirable as long as inhabiting it doesn't pervert the substance of your own organization's values. You've also come upon yet another reason why to resist the temptation to create a canned, one-version-fits-all presentation of your outfit as an applicant for resources.

Blending Resources

The weakest funding applications are those that represent a proposed effort supported by nothing more than the funds requested in the budget, thereby rendering it wholly dependent on as yet unsecured resources. Counteract this and add to the sense of organizational soundness by addressing how you intend to assemble a mixture of assets to combine with those you seek in the proposal in the next section, labeled Blending Resources.

For example, if your nonprofit has been the beneficiary of a special fundraising event conducted by a service organization, you have the means to use the net proceeds, or a portion, as a contribution to be used with the dollars requested to carry out the proposed program.

Or if yours is the occasional organization that has managed to open a retail operation, where income exceeds expenses and revenue becomes available to support general operations, you also have the ability to propose blending some profit with requested external funds.

Demonstrating how you have secured non-cash, in-kind contributions of volunteered services, managed to locate donated space in which to operate, using donated furnishings and equipment as part of the proposed effort is certainly another measure of a tenacious, creative organization. There is a dollar value to be reflected in your budget for every form of such in-kind support based on what you would pay to acquire such resources in the commercial marketplace.

You may have also discovered that businesses, large and small, often the objects of our attention in seeking support, are less inclined to part with the cash they so prize, but are willing to impart a sense of their good corporate citizenship by offering non-cash support. If your organization has benefitted accordingly, allocate such resources for use in your proposed effort.

There is yet another aspect to the beneficial impulse to blend resources when looking for ways to support the efforts presented in funding proposals. This finds us approaching more than one source of possible funding at the same time. There are several variations on this theme, and each is derived from what our research of external funders divulges.

You might, for example, necessarily approach more than one source of possible support when it is apparent that no one source will be able or willing to provide all the funds sought in your proposal.

You also might segment your request for funds to approach several prospects that confine their willingness to make resources available for strictly defined categories. One example would be learning that a particular entity only provides funds to support equipment purchase, and your proposed effort includes the need for such outlays. The multiple funder approach kicks in when directing a proposal for hardware to that funder, while looking elsewhere for support for other project categories such as staff salaries or even hard to come by general support.

Here's a shrewdly developed iteration of the tactics being considered—this would find you approaching multiple funding sources with essentially the same proposal, even going so far as to ask each source approached for all the funds for your project. You would, in effect, be asking for more funds than needed to maximize the prospect of securing those you need, and no, you're not likely to get more than you need.

If you're thinking that this makes no sense because it offers each of the funders approached a reason to more easily deny your request since, after all, you have alternative prospects in the eyes of each, here's some rethinking.

First, would you forsake the canniness of discovering and approaching more than one legitimate prospect just to eliminate the possibility of being turned down more than once? Bear in mind that the approach to funders being recommended here is predicated on your careful research to select them, not anything like scattering proposals all over the funding landscape, something already described as idiotic.

Next, funding organizations don't need excuses to turn down your proposals—they do it all the time, whether you have one proposal or several out there for scrutiny. This is why a thick skin is necessary when you seek resources. Declinations far exceed the good news in the broadly defined funding arena, even when the very best proposal you can imagine having created is out there representing your intentions.

And finally you may be able to distinguish your organization by setting aside the tendency to worry that funders always look for ways to torpedo proposals. Rather, you deal out proposals based on the conviction that their excellence deserves wider consideration. This is a heady tactic reinforced by the care with which you select funding sources, the substance of how you bring life to your proposal in its creation and its movement out your door, along with the belief that your proposal remains viable even if it is declined.

Maintaining Continuity

This resource-developing business never ceases for people in nonprofits. Mindful of this, and that most external funding is episodic and impermanent, it falls on your organization to continue pursuing resources until its mission is accomplished.

This is a matter that needs attention under the heading, Maintaining Continuity, the most striking aspect of which is the extent to which you convey your organization's intention to pick up where proposed funding leaves off; to continue the quest to complete its mission, rarely with any guaranteed ways of doing so. This will find you strategizing every bit as tenaciously and creatively as when you described blending resources, only this time describing your tactics with the future in mind.

You're likely to look into prospects for more stable long-term income-generating options. This might find you finally being serious about a membership development program you've discussed repeatedly. Since direct mail solicitation , if successful—a big if—is the most potent way to get unrestricted money into your coffers, maybe it's time to begin testing it. Or maybe your proposal would relate your intentions to unearth or devote funds to conduct a feasibility study for a business where profit not subject to unrelated business income tax would become a source of ongoing support for your mission-couched efforts.

Just as evaluation represents a way to protect a proposed investment, so too does addressing this issue. This is because your forward thinking makes it possible for a would-be financial backer to appreciate that the one-time funding being proposed serves as leverage to move your organization forward into a larger, longer term sense of its intended progress.

The time always comes in proposal development when you have to translate what you have articulated into the dollars needed to make it possible. So we turn to the Budget and Budget Narrative.

Budget and Budget Narrative

Since, more often than not, you are likely to be focusing on some sort of specific project for which money is sought, the budget layout following is a two-column categorical line item budget format.

Such a framework would not work if you were seeking funds for some type of capital project—construction, renovation, equipment purchase—but you should find that entities willing to support such projects will also supply the required format.

Nor would a line item format be suitable in a request for general operating support, the nonprofit resource seekers version of manna from heaven. In this case, you would most probably need to present an annual organizational budget, including projected income and expenses, and very likely financial audit findings.

It is not necessary now to delve into the finer points of budget making when considering this incontestably important element in a proposal. Some who get a gleam in their eyes when it comes to working numbers would suggest budgeting is a subject unto itself. So I'll leave it to you to find such mad geniuses and bring them into your fold. And, there is always your trusty bookkeeper...

There are, nonetheless, some aspects of budget building that are worth discussing here. Take padding budgets, for example. You may have acquired a certain sagacity when dealing with funders, probably grant makers who always appear to operate on the basis of whacking any budget request they see. So, were you to indicate that you pad your requests to anticipate this, who could quibble?

Nonetheless, you should appreciate that the budgets you work with are a reflection of your organization's ethos. An accurate, detailed budget for funding seems only right if yours is an excellent, well-constructed proposal. This way, if and when it comes to negotiating a budget, you have an unassailable basis for pointing out the implication of cuts and how they will change the texture of the proposed program, thereby defending what you've submitted.

Be prepared to be exposed to another facet of business as usual, the almost relentless and wholly unwarranted negative view some funders hold of administrative costs likely to be part of any budget you fashion. This translates into ludicrous administrative cost percentage caps, such as those stipulating no more than 15% to 20%. The profane implications are that your organization ought not include skilled people or seek resources to compensate them for their expertise.

Along with clearly detailing the responsibilities of administrative staff in your Proposed Program Strategy, there isn't much more to offer to counter such prejudice than once again formulating an accurate, detailed budget and narrative, along with job descriptions, to be used to justify personnel excellence.

We're nudging into the nexus between what a budget reveals and what your proposal represents. Specifically, there should be a vivid relationship between the budget and three previously reviewed elements of your proposal:

- THE PROPOSED PROGRAM STRATEGY, *because this is where most of the costs you want the prospective investor to underwrite will appear*
- EVALUATION METHODS, *because an intentional, albeit subjective, assessment is an integral part of any work you undertake to pursue your mission, and the costs of associated personnel and activities belong in the budget*
- *And* BLENDING RESOURCES, *because this is where non-requested assets to be matched with those you seek are described, the dollar values of which will be displayed in the Other Sources column of the budget format*

Remember, if funded, your budget out-the-door moves from a projection to a contract by which your organization will, in part, be judged. So you need to be accountable by being able to track and document your outlays as they are made—bookkeeper stuff.

Here is the plain vanilla line item budget format suggested for your use:

I. PERSONNEL	REQUESTED	OTHER SOURCES
A. Salaries and Wages		
B. Benefits		
C. Staff Development		
D. Consultants and Contract Services		
SUB-TOTAL		
II. NON-PERSONNEL	**REQUESTED**	**OTHER SOURCES**
A. Space Costs		
B. Rental, Lease, and Purchase of Equipment		
C. Consumable Supplies		
D. Travel		
E. Telecommunications		
F. Other Costs		
SUB-TOTAL		
GRAND TOTAL		

(Indirect Costs, as a % of all direct costs or some portion, may be added. See Federal OMB Circular A-122 for guidance.)

Summary

And now the Summary comes into play, only possible after you complete your proposal. You can't summarize what you haven't articulated.

Its parts, taken from the proposal, are presented ***BRIEFLY***, paraphrasing:

- *Who we are*
- *What concerns us*
- *Resolution of what concerns us*
- *How we will bring about such resolution*
- *How long it will take, how much it will cost, and how much we want from you*

When complete, the summary—again, no more than a paragraph or two—will move to the front end of a proposal reorganized for presentation purposes. This confirms its importance as a lead-in to the details to follow in your entire document. When you visualize someone taking up your proposal, you can hope this snapshot entices them to read further.

Further, this summary of a detailed and thorough proposal offers the added value as the basis for being expanded into the document some funders require prior to or in lieu of a full proposal. Usually labeled Letters of Inquiry or Letters of Intent, you should always treat them as pre-proposal proposals. Also, lean on the summary when you summon up the gumption to present a promising funding source with a brief, unsolicited, off-cycle concept paper.

Devising the one or two pages that will mark any of these types of documents is a cinch when you can amplify the summary. To repeat, you can only have such a summary with which to work if, and only if, you have completed the substantial proposal development process that, lo and behold, results in something to summarize.

Once you have worked through and built your proposal, remind yourselves that this process was informed by pulling apart the presentation format initially discussed and itemized. This means you convert what you created in the left-hand column on *PAGE 66* into the format in the right-hand column for presentation. And, when it comes time to send a complete package out the door, electronic or otherwise, your proposal is likely to be accompanied by a cover letter and attachments.

The cover letter can be a strategic instrument if you treat it with the importance it deserves. To build it, use your letterhead, complete with logo, and a list of your board with a one-word description of each member's skill set, occupation, or affiliation in the left margin.

Start the letter with the proper personal salutation, not To Whom it May Concern, followed by a repeat of the summary from the proposal it accompanies. (This is solid strategy because it is possible for the letter to be separated and walked around for viewing as a mini-proposal when it arrives at its destination.)

After the recurring summary, then the signatory, who should be the chairperson of your outfit's board of directors, can weigh in to verify full board authorization to submit the proposal, something made all the more impressive if this person also discloses having participated in its development.

Counteract the natural tendency to slump once your proposal is out the door by indicating in your cover letter that someone will follow up to see if anything else should be sent to augment the proposal, and whether protocol includes a meeting or site visit. Getting a face-to-face meeting likely depends on a combination of your reasonable persistence and, most probably, the quirks of organizational behavior from your hoped-for partner.

Do not, in any event, wait to hear from the funder. Your proposed efforts deserve much more than such passivity. Your proposal, undoubtedly one of many, may have been misplaced. Or maybe the person assigned to review it is on sick leave. Or... Why would you entertain and undertake the substantial work to argue for support only to go limp once you transpose it to and convey it by the written word? Make the call, or send the email.

As for attachments to your proposal, combine whatever the organization you are approaching requires—the letter of determination from the IRS, for example, or most recent audit findings—and those items you judge will enhance your proposal; letters of endorsement and job descriptions were previously mentioned. An annual report, program brochure, evidence of favorable media coverage, or a judiciously produced audio/visual item would also be suitable additions.

When the time comes that you see fit to leave this book, get into action and gather others to develop your proposal, *THE KEYS TO DEVELOPING POWERFUL FUNDING PROPOSALS* in the *TOOL KIT SECTION* is there to help. Meanwhile, take a brief look at the work of others learning to build proposals for inspiration and, very possibly, a measure of humility.

CHAPTER SIX

TAKEAWAYS

Here is an overview of your new proposal framework, in the order you'll build it, and what each section is aiming to do.

1. Case for Needed Change

- Verifying and describing the quality of life challenges among the people for whom your organization exists
- Showing a clear understanding of the factors that contribute to such challenges
- Leveraging research-based data to corroborate and bolster your case, if available, including demographic research, studies, academic research

2. Defining Participant Success

- Showing prospective funders/investors a true cost-benefit analysis of your program strategy to follow
- Specifying the number of people intended to benefit from your efforts
- Including modified success indicators that adapt to time constraints of impermanent funding sources
- Defining participant success in incremental stages or phases (to help avoid over-promising)

3. Proposed Program Strategy

- Using previously specified measures of success as the starting point for program tactics
- Highlighting your collaboration with the people you're aiming to uplift with your projecting

- A timeline of activities or tasks, typically across the span of a year, including long-term plans to show the continuation of your efforts beyond your proposal
- Specifying staff, materials and facilities, and outlining project management and any collaboration with other organizations

4. Evaluation Methods

- Accounting for quality of work as it unfolds and subsequent impact
- Outlining when and how often how you will stay connected with the people running the program and the people affected by it
- Indicating how you will measure impact, any outside support to help you, and how you intend to analyze your findings
- Disseminating your findings to the array of people and organizations connected to your cause

5. Applicant for Funding

- Showing your capabilities as an organization to deliver the core elements of your proposal
- As a new nonprofit, highlighting the skills and experience of your founding members, or documenting the urgency of the situation you are proposing to tackle

- As an established organization, elevating acknowledgement from other organizations, and the community you serve
- Using a mix of media to share your story of impact, including video, photos, testimonials, and letters of endorsement
- Outlining fiscal soundness, who's managing all the money and any audit results to reinforce your trustworthiness

6. Blending Resources

- Including a mixture of current assets, from in-kind contributions to fundraising proceeds as an inducement to requested funding
- Delineating any funding from other sources, current or potential, for aspects of the proposed program
- Distinguishing your organization by unabashedly seeking funds from several potential funders, conveying confidence in the legitimacy of your proposal

7. Maintaining Continuity

- Describing options to pick up where proposed funding leaves off, to continue the quest to complete your mission
- Including all your current funding strategies

- Exploring new ideas, such as testing and refining direct mail, targeting native advertising, or even conducting a feasibility study for a business
- Demonstrating forward-thinking to convince financial backers that their one-time funding would help drive for long-term progress

8. Budget and Budget Narrative

- Including a detailed budget and narrative, along with job descriptions, to be used to justify personnel excellence
- Reinforcing the relationship between the budget and the details in the Proposed Program Strategy, Evaluation Methods, and Blending Resources sections
- Presenting an annual organizational budget, including projected income and expenses

9. Summary

- Kicking off your proposal with a compelling and compact overview -- presented in no more than a couple of paragraphs
- Who you are
- What concerns you
- Resolution of what concerns you

- How you will bring about such resolution
- How long it will take
- How much it will cost and how much you're seeking

Almost Done!

- Reorganize what you've built to read as follows:

  SUMMARY

  APPLICANT FOR FUNDING

  CASE FOR NEEDED CHANGE

  DEFINING PARTICIPANT SUCCESS

  PROGRAM STRATEGY

  EVALUATION METHODS

  BLENDING RESOURCES

  MAINTAINING CONTINUITY

  BUDGET AND NARRATIVE

- Write a convincing cover letter.
- Include all of your attachments (e.g. videos, audit information, etc.).

After It's Sent

- Don't call it a day just yet! Always, always, always follow up.

CHAPTER SEVEN

HELPFUL EXAMPLES

- A Story of Proposal Writing Gone Awry *(and What Should Have Happened)*
- An Incisive, Persuasive Letter Proposal
- An Effective One-Pager

The notion of creating a proposal prototype suffers when considering the range of possibilities for which funding proposals are presented. The following subjects, in a Foundation Center publication under the category of grantmaking, would not seem to lend themselves to a one-proposal-fits-all slant.

> *Abuse prevention, bioethics, community development, dispute resolution, environment, family planning, gays/lesbians, hospices, immigrants/refugees, journalism and publishing, leadership development, museums, Native Americans, offenders/ex-offenders, public health, rural development, speech and hearing centers, transportation, urban community development, voter education, youth services*

Nevertheless, the desire to find ways you might expedite reproducing funding proposals is understandable—as long as you use common sense when considering options.

For example, we previously discussed creating the legitimate version of a boilerplate proposal as the base from which more specific documents could be constructed, but only by using the strategy and tactics this book values.

And, there are some other creative options to consider on the way into hatching your proposal-in-the-making. You might, for example, try asking accessible funders to share copies of previously funded proposals for perusal. Some will do this. The idea is to learn what you can from a successful scenario. This makes sense, as long as you use common sense with what you've learned from what you've read. Such was not evident in the following true story.

The staff of a mental health organization, in its quest for funding, had asked the intended funder if there were other applications they could look over while preparing to come forward with their own proposal. These were made available. Long story short, the would-be grant maker declined the organization's initial application. This was because the proposal did not sufficiently document issues prevalent in the local community, while proposing a range of mental health strategies. In other words, the program techniques described in other proposals were mimicked—after all, they had been funded before. But this made no sense in the absence of clarity about why they were needed in the first place in a particular community setting, or dreadfully named catchment area, at the time. (Second time was the charm, proposal funded.)

Such a reasonable situation as just described, and the learning it illustrates, are supplanted altogether too often by indefensibly cutting corners. This happens time and again when getting money is the sole motivation for generating a proposal. When this is so, it follows that any funded proposal is a model proposal, so all you need to do is find one and mimic it. Leading from this absurd premise, and pandering to those unwilling or unaware of how to be earnest in this work, there are even books for sale chock full of dubious samples of "winning" proposals. Let the proposal writer beware...

Rather than hollow illusions, what follows is a mix of three real life examples of the work of people teamed together to improve their skills while learning the craft of proposal development. Each is instructive in its own way, as you will see. On the one hand, you will see the unadorned reality of how hard it is to translate interpersonal communication into words, and on the other, you will also see how well it can be done.

The first proposal includes my numbered comments as the proverbial fly on the wall. The idea is to pique your imagination about what might evolve if the writers were to return to the drawing board, so to say. The second is an excellent letter proposal for funding, with laudatory comments. And, the third , another product to emerge from a previous training program, is effective because of the economy of its presentation of key proposal elements.

There are fictitious substitutions for real names throughout since I grabbed each product unbeknownst to the authors after completing a training program.

EXAMPLE ONE

A Story of Proposal Writing Gone Awry

INTRODUCTION

❶ Consolidated Community Centers (CCS) is a private not-for-profit United Way agency that offers services for youth, family and senior citizens in the City of Macrotown, Anystate. The mission of CCS is "to improve the quality of life for people at the neighborhood level, especially in the neighborhoods where the problems are most severe and the help most needed."

Two of CCS's facilities, Cosmopolitan Center and Churchview Center, have been in operation since 1944. In 1959 letters were filed with the state of Anystate joining these two independent entities to form Consolidated Community Centers. Today, through a series of centers, with programs including after-school and evening programs for teens, daycare for working parents, a food and clothing program for the poor, and nutrition and socialization programs for seniors, CCS provides comprehensive services in three neighborhood locations.

CCS has been the trailblazer❷ service provider of programs and services to seniors in Sprawly County. In 1977, CCS was the sole provider of senior services, being responsible for the formation of the first senior center congregate meals program. The agency's executive structure includes a board of directors, an executive director, four program directors, and 17 other full-time and nine part-time paid employees. The agency depends

(and What Should Have Happened)

❶ This is where a mission statement belongs. Whenever one is offered, however, the fly looks for evidence of progress in meeting the mission—some mission-accomplished statements, if you will.

Nothing that follows in this proposal suggests to me that this organization, for as long as it has existed, has much to say about impact among the so-called senior citizens for whom it exists. Lots of information about the organization's activities, but busy ain't necessarily successful.

❷ "Trailblazer" and "sole" service provider—without reference to significance, these terms don't mean much.

on community volunteers on a daily basis, especially in the senior center program.

The agency is funded by United Way of Sprawly County, the County Area Agency on Aging, Sprawly Children and Youth Services, the State Department of Education, and private contributions. The combined agency budget for CCS for the last year was $987,000. (See Appendix A ❸ for Board of Directors Directory and Appendix B for 1997-98 Annual Report.)

PROBLEM STATEMENT (CASE FOR NEEDED CHANGE)

According to the most recent Census Bureau figures, 29% of the population of the City of Macrotown is over the age of 65.❹ It constitutes one of the largest urban concentrations of elderly people in the state, as well as in the Southwest. The senior population in south Macrotown has access to the Consolidated Community Centers Southside Senior Citizens Center, currently located in a small rental space shared with a civic organization. In a 70' x 55' single-activity room, the center provides programs such as: arts and crafts including bingo, dance group sessions, hooking rugs, and daily meals.

Because of restrictions on the availability of space, the center can only operate six hours per weekday. (See photo, Appendix C.) Program participants have expressed a need for more socialization, recreation, and information activities.

However, the center is unable to implement these needs ❺ under the current restrictive conditions. We need a new building to house a lineup of expanded services. Over the more than twenty years that we have been working with our senior

❸ Consigning the board to Appendix A relegates them to inconsequential status rather than highlighting their accomplishments for the organization. Nothing is offered about the exemplary work of all the staff. Just mentioning that they're around is underwhelming. What is the difference those valued volunteers make on the quality of the program?

Nothing said about the community's support for the organization. No evidence of positive media treatment. There is an impressive array of additional funders, but without connecting the dollars to community improvement, it loses some zing.

❹ Lots of old folks. What's the point? I might conclude that many of them are wealthy. For those involved with the one community center, they're apparently socializing in pleasant enough ways, are they not?

If the idea is that "program participants have expressed a need ..." why not personalize this and include some quotes that bring to life the impact in the quality of their lives? Rather than reading like an urgent challenge, this reads like an inconvenience, where a move to a new facility would be pleasant, not essential. It would not be difficult to conclude that the possibly well-to-do seniors should pay for the improvement in the present discomfort, thereby weakening the argument for funding.

The use of the photo to convey difficult circumstances makes sense.

population, we have developed an array of activities and programs, which has greatly reduced its needs.

Nevertheless, we confirm the sentiment of the area seniors that the center has simply outgrown its site. CCS wishes to expand its services since it receives far more requests for assistance services than it can presently handle. Many of these requests come from seniors who live alone and struggle with insurance dilemmas, health issues, finance management, and social and nutritional needs. The area agency has also identified these needs among the county's senior population and asserts that there are many elderly living a lonely existence who could benefit from a more functional facility and expanded service program.

It is imperative to acquire these new facilities because the elderly population generally lead isolated lives, live on fixed income, face diminished physical abilities, and are increasingly dependent. These conditions could be more fully addressed and alleviated by the institutional service and programs that CCS and its collaborators could offer in a new building. ❻

For five years, ❼ CCS and the area agency on aging have sought to relocate and expand their services at the request of seniors. Other senior services providers have expressed interest in developing a consortium (see Appendix D) to operate a geriatric healthcare center to offer germane services, including insurance counseling, health services, prevention and education instruction case management, and geriatric physician services. Not only would South Macrotown neighborhood seniors benefit from an expanded facility and programming, but seniors throughout Sprawly County would be served.

❺ What in the name of all that is nonprofit does it mean to "implement needs"? This seems to indicate that we're going to make certain that we have these needs, when surely what is meant is that the center is unable to meet such needs. Add to these muddled words now the absolutely obvious shift to "needing" a building. Finally, this is followed by the connotation that all activities the applicant carries out reduce needs. I wonder why they labeled this section the problem statement. The various versions of neediness serve to make the concept unclear if not useless.

Now we see that perhaps some of the target group are not faring so well. We don't wish upon these people the struggles mentioned here, but if this is what's really going on, then there ought to be more documentation to indicate that these are seniors who don't do so well when left on their own, and that they are looking for help.

If the area agency is involved in verifying need, they'd better show up somewhere in this proposal as doing something about the situation.

❻ What continues to nag, however, is why the applicant concludes that a building is needed.

It seems bizarre to imagine that they are withholding services for people described as isolated and dependent just because there is no new building, but that's what's being conveyed in the proposal now.

❼ Five years!! I guess the point is to show how long they've been searching. All the fly can think about is dereliction of duty. If the needs are as compelling as they would have us believe, not coming up with some previous

South Macrotown, the center of the county's population base of seniors, would be an ideal site for a new facility, combining a senior center and geriatric healthcare center, which would allow participating agencies to fulfill their mission of improved support services to senior citizens. ❽

There is a strong sense of community among our seniors. In an effort to show their commitment to the project, they have organized fundraising events, including the first ever recorded senior citizens car wash, quilt raffles, bake sales, and craft bazaars. They appreciate CCS's efforts on their behalf and want to contribute to a project, which they perceive as essential to the quality of their lives.

OBJECTIVES (OUTCOMES)

The outcome is to construct a new building. This new expanded facility, combined with a geriatric healthcare component, will allow seniors throughout the county to participate in a range of activities designed to meet their stated needs. ❾

METHODS

To actualize the construction of the proposed new building, a consortium of providers is in place which will operate the geriatric healthcare to be located within the proposed South Macrotown Senior Citizens Center.

Funding for the geriatric healthcare center has been secured under a separate grant awarded to the area agency on aging. The funding is contingent upon the construction of the proposed new facility which will be owned and managed by CCS.

approach short of a building to meet them compromises the organization's credibility, at a minimum.

❽ Now there's a shift into a proposed consortium, but nothing is said about why it's needed other than to offer more services. The problem statement should clearly answer the question of why more services are needed, and do so by getting back to what confronts a known number or group of so-called seniors. (I haven't counted, but the use of the word senior here is enervating and just may be a bit condescending. Be careful with labels. You never know who might be reading your stuff. In this instance, it might be an age-wizened fly on the wall.) See to it that the people being categorized agree with such a characterization.

❾ No, no, a thousand times no!! The outcome is not to build a building. The building is a means to an end. If the building is the objective, then it could be said that these folks were successful if they had a standing building without one senior in it. The objective is to meet the compelling needs of people—or better—the challenges facing those for whom this organization was created. The proposal writers certainly haven't let us lose sight of who that is, although it gets to the point where it seems the applicant needs the seniors rather than the opposite. If there were a greater sense of living, breathing people in the preceding section of the proposal as well as here, the fly on the wall might not be so moved to such speculation.

Notice how it says that the building will lead to "activities designed" to meet stated needs. Those needs never were stated. Because this is so, the proposal architects are not able to present "objectives" as outcomes describing

CCS, as the umbrella agency and project manager, has determined the cost of the building project to be $743,000. CCS has obtained first option on a construction site for the proposed new facility, architectural drawings, and construction estimates. Partial funding from the Whynot Foundation in the amount of $245,000 has been awarded and a commitment of long-term financing has been secured.

A local medical group has expressed interest in leasing space for its medical practice. This tenant would complement the senior-oriented programs provided by the center. This rental income will offset long-term maintenance cost and construction debt associated with the project. ❿

EVALUATION

The best evidence of our accomplishment is a building that adequately houses the finest available support services and programs which, combined, make the Center one where an older adult and his/her family can be secure in the meeting of their needs.

Already a provider of volume services and activities to seniors, CCS's construction of a more functional center will enable a greater number of activities and services to take place simultaneously.

The addition of a geriatric healthcare management component will attract additional seniors from throughout the county.

As a United Way agency, CCS is required to track the unduplicated number of participants served. This will provide evi-

the benefits for participants, or the needs met, to use their numbing concept.

⑩ There's an inconsistency because previously they said interest in developing a consortium had been expressed; now we have one in place. By the same token, the concept of such collaboration seems sensible, although you would want a proposal to include what program responsibilities each of the participating agencies would take when describing the proposed methods here.

At this point we're getting ahead of ourselves. This proposal seeks money for erecting a building, so this section should describe activities related to the construction process. This should include expanding on the paragraph that mentions first option, drawings, and estimates. More details and a non-calendar specific proposed schedule of construction-related activities should be included.

Also recommended is an attachment to the proposal, cited in this section, to describe the anticipated program and staffing configuration to kick in after the building is finished. It could also be mentioned under Future Funding as a focus for continued resource development.

All the references to additional funding commitments—powerful indeed—should be discussed in what we have previously described as Blending Resources in our proposal development format. This proposal included no such section, although there is a discussion of future funding, as you'll see. Reference to the medical group's participation should be included in that section.

dence of the increase of the county's senior population utilizing the facility. In addition, the Department of Social Work at the University of ChurnEmOut has developed an instrument to measure the extent to which seniors' needs are met. We plan to contract the department as consultant evaluators to collect and analyze data, and report results on a semi-annual basis to our board of directors, consortium administrators, and overseeing agencies. ⓫

FUTURE FUNDING

We project that the annual maintenance and utilities costs for the building will be $79,000. Each service provider participating will contribute 4% of its annual budget toward these costs. In addition, rental income will be derived from a tenant to offset long-term maintenance costs and construction debt associated with the project. ⓬

BUDGET

It is based on the projected total of $743,000 to construct the new building. This cost is reduced by the $245,000 grant in place from the foundation and the long-term financing mentioned previously, a loan for $286,000, resulting in a request for a grant of $212,000. ⓭

⓫ The fly suggests that the best evidence is satisfied customers. What specific evaluation activities will be established to find out if people are getting their needs met? Once again, the building, activities and services overshadow people. The throw-in about the geriatric care attracting more people is an unsupported assumption. Further, it says nothing about how to assess the impact of services if more people do show up.

The United Way requirement is nothing more than a head count, which is only one aspect of evaluation.

If the university has the instrument, as indicated, how it will be used should be further described here. A reader gets no sense of the proposed methods for evaluating the project's impact.

And, nothing is mentioned about how the construction process will be monitored, another fundamental aspect of evaluation.

⓬ As far as this goes, it's well done. It would be strengthened if there were dollar values given for the 4% provider outlays and the proposed rental income, so a reader could see the total offset of the projected annual costs.

⓭ This is fine. In a request for capital funding such as this is, the budget is straightforward. More detailed cost estimates in the Methods section would allow a reader to see where money is allocated. On the other hand, they could have itemized the construction activities in the Methods section and then articulated the costs for such activities here. The point is that the budget should reflect the costs associated with the proposed activities.

EXAMPLE TWO

An Incisive, Persuasive Letter Proposal

It is gratifying, and perhaps even edifying, to look at proposal writing of a commendable sort, therefore the well-conceived letter proposal that follows. Best seen as a Letter of Inquiry or Letter of Intent, it was composed and shared following a training program. Facts have been humor-doctored to maintain anonymity, but the themes are intact.

Offering a sound argument for support, this document also demonstrates that one of the true measures of creativity in writing of this sort lies in distilling content, a skill not easily acquired. Some features:

- *Important information is specified in just under two pages, supporting the notion that it would be read in its entirety.*

- *There is a good jolt of applicant credibility, including willingness to put its own resources on the table to induce the requested funds*

- *The reason for funding is reasonably presented, verifying that health-related challenges confront people in a target area.*

- *This leads to an equally reasonable solution to their difficulties insofar as those previously in jeopardy are projected to experience a preferable, even life-saving alternative.*

- *Finally, the applicant proposes to take responsibility for following up to see how the potential partnership might evolve.*

It's also apparent that the letter proposal features a cohesive applicant for funding. The author was well-grounded in the organization and its work, only possible if she had taken time to involve other people, staff and community members among them, to learn the organization, in effect. A lesson for us all...

Ms. Raquel F. McMeans
Administrative Officer
The Infrastructure Foundation
1042 East Little Bear Way
Postland, WA 98000
Dear Ms. McMeans:

Children's Hospital, Inc., Washington's only full-service rural pediatric hospital, plans to meet the needs of underserved children through a pediatric intensive care unit to be operated on an outreach basis, providing ambulance service within a 75-mile radius. The estimated cost is $104,274 of which Children's is requesting $75,774 for moving equipment.

A 100-bed facility, Children's meets patient needs through provision of acute care and a full range of rehabilitative services on an out- and in-patient basis. It is fully accredited by the Joint Commission on the Accreditation of Hospitals and licensed by all appropriate city and state agencies. It is also a medical teaching hospital affiliated with the medical schools of Case Northern University and Washington State College. (A copy of the Letter of Determination from the IRS demonstrating tax-exempt, nonprofit status is included.) The hospital's board of directors, a committee of which participated in planning this initial approach for funding, will assume a proper role in helping to support the project in the future, consistent with its active fundraising stance for all Children's work.

Currently, only 22 of Washington's 48 counties have office-based pediatricians. And in the proposed four-county service area, with no such arrangement, the birth and infant mortality rates exceed the national average. This is verified by local data as well as information from the State Department of Health. The target area lacks facilities such as the one being proposed, and in two counties, according to their local statistics, birth defects exceed national and comparable county norms. Related characteristics for the target area conspire to immobilize those underserved. These include a high level of illiteracy, a high percentage of rural poor, including several hundred non-reservation Native Americans, low incomes from seasonal agricultural activities, and nearly non-existent public transportation services.

The proposed project will replace makeshift, limited, and poorly equipped facilities already overtaxed to meet demands upon them. As planned, the project will enable Children's staff to quickly transport ill children, newborns with critical birth defects, and children hurt by accident or abuse to a facility established to save their lives.

Children's proposes to finance and orchestrate the pediatric outreach project through 1) the use of already existing space and two staff members, 2) a local foundation grant of $28,500 to be paid for start-up personnel costs on receipt of funds to cover the cost of equipment, and 3) receipt of the subject grant from the Infrastructure Foundation for such purpose.

To maximize the prospects for success in this start-up project, Children's staff has had initial discussions about funding possibilities with representatives of the Thus and So Foundation, and the chief executive officer of locally headquartered Wondrous/Malevolent Industries. While no specific commitments are in place, we anticipate that more such discussions will occur, in particular after the proposed project is up and running.

The estimated annual cost to operate the project after initial funding is $225,000, of which a minimum of $100,000 can be supported in the hospital's present budget. Additional operational grants will be sought for the balance of the initial year of providing service. We anticipate that the unit will be largely self-supporting through annual giving commitments and third-party reimbursements thereafter.

Abstracts of relevant information from the hospital's operating budget are included, along with a brief chronicle of Children's development over twenty years from a 50-bed rehabilitation center to its present status.

If more information is needed to add to the quality of this initial request, you have only to request as much. I will follow up with a phone call within three weeks to seek your advice for further action in promoting this partnership between our organizations.

Sincerely yours,

Lance Boyler,

Executive Director

EXAMPLE THREE

An Effective One-Pager

There is beauty in brevity when one reads many funding proposals. A team of participants developed what follows as a fine example of making essential points emphasized in a training program in less than two pages. Understand that this team created a fully articulated proposal over several days, and distilled what is here from that document. It would be the basis for a Letter of Intent or Letter of Inquiry by many funders. You'll find annotations derived from our proposal development framework in italics following each section of the document.

Somewhat Suburban City Schools (SSCS) Elementary District (K-8) established in 1915 serves 3,300 students representing over 16 language groups at nine school sites. Three of the district's schools have been designated as State Distinguished Schools, and one has received the prestigious Purple Ribbon Award. *(Introducing a credible Applicant for Funding)*

Currently, students leave the eighth grade without the technological skills needed to succeed in high school. Fully 40% of these students have no access to computers outside school. Further, a large percentage of talented teachers have entered the SSCS system untrained in technology. Both situations reflect the speed with which technology applications have appeared, and the understandable gap in grasping them within the fabric of public education. With the introduction of more computer hardware at each site within the district, there is an attendant necessity to increase technical support to maintain full operation and usefulness. *(Making the Case for Change based on target groups' needs)*

To respond to these realities, and as part of the current SSCS strategic planning, teachers, students, parents, and community members established competency benchmarks to be accomplished by students and teachers at the conclusion of a four-year technology implementation schedule. A technology taskforce that will continue to oversee activities as they unfold has refined these standards. *(Establishing Measurable Outcomes/defining success in the form of competency benchmarks, although who and how many will accomplish these is not specified; establishing a basis for Ongoing Evaluation through the task force.)*

Implementation over four years is marked by the following tactics: a three-tiered staff development and training program to include parent education and training; a computer and software lending program; a literacy learning link; peer coaching network; and a portable instruction learning of technology (PILOT) lab. *(Presenting an appropriate Program Strategy)*

SSCS is deeply committed to meeting this technology literacy challenge. The project is envisioned as a possible model for other school districts confronting the same issues. As such, the district has assigned office personnel to assist with implementation and coordination of continued community collaboration. Budget totals to complete the project are $ for year one, $ for year two, $ for year three; and $ for the fourth year. The district seeks $ for the first year to be matched by in-kind goods and services, the value of which is $. *(Additional Resources to be leveraged with proposed funds; Maintaining Project Continuity over four years.)*

These imperfect, encapsulated examples of real life endeavors among the many who go after resources for their nonprofits serve to reinforce the value of the strategy and tactics presented for your consideration here. A participant put it well as we wrapped up a training program, sharing his realization that the proposal takes care of itself if you do the needed internal work and, as he put it, get your organization's thinking clear. He went on to say that a proposal emerges from such a process if and when it is appropriate. This is wisdom of a special sort.

Draw your own conclusion by embracing a similar clarifying internal development process when you tackle the next proposal. Remember, the consistent, persistent theme throughout here has been to broaden the application of potent principles for building effective funding proposals and use them in strengthening the organization seeking funds at the same time. Once again, think of this as developing your organization by developing its proposals.

All the creativity and internal strengthening to build compelling funding proposals from competent nonprofits leads to the broad realm of prospective benefactors, the ones with the assets we want. Let's turn our attention to where to unearth these funding partners in the making.

CHAPTER EIGHT

THE FUNDING

A world of possibilities.

Here we go:

- *FEDERAL GRANTS FROM WASHINGTON, D.C.*
- *FEDERAL GRANTS THROUGH FEDERAL REGIONAL OFFICES*
- *FEDERAL GRANTS THROUGH SINGLE STATE AGENCIES/STATE PLANNING AGENCIES*
- *DIRECT FEDERAL LOANS*
- *FEDERAL LOAN GUARANTEES*
- *FEDERAL INSURANCE PROGRAMS*
- *SPECIALIZED SERVICES/FEDERAL PERSONNEL ON LOAN*
- *POSSIBLE FEDERAL TRAINING PROGRAMS*
- *FEDERAL CONTRACTS*
- *STATE APPROPRIATIONS FOR GRANTS AND/OR CONTRACTS*
- *OFFICES OF ELECTED OFFICIALS*
- *STAFFED GRANTMAKING FOUNDATIONS (NATIONAL GRANTS/ PROGRAM-RELATED INVESTMENTS (PRIS)*
- *STAFFED GRANTMAKING FOUNDATIONS (LOCAL GRANTS/ GIFTS)*
- *STAFFED OPERATING FOUNDATIONS (LOCAL AND NATIONAL)*
- *UNSTAFFED GRANTMAKING FOUNDATIONS*
- *GRANTMAKING PUBLIC CHARITIES, INCLUDING COMMUNITY FOUNDATIONS*
- *CORPORATE FOUNDATIONS*
- *DIRECT CORPORATE GIVING—HEADQUARTERS, REGIONS, BRANCHES*

- *EMPLOYEE-DRIVEN GIVING; EMPLOYEE MATCHING PROGRAMS; TRADE ASSOCIATIONS*
- *UNIONS*
- *LOCAL BUSINESSES*
- *FEDERATED GIVING PROGRAMS—UNITED WAY; JEWISH FEDERATION*
- *PAYROLL DEDUCTION PROGRAMS—COMBINED FEDERAL CAMPAIGN; STATE GOVERNMENT CAMPAIGNS; UNITED WAY DONOR OPTION; INDEPENDENT CORPORATE PLANS*
- *CIVIC/PROFESSIONAL/SERVICE ORGANIZATIONS (CLUBS SUCH AS ELKS, MOOSE, JUNIOR LEAGUE, ROTARY, SOROPTIMIST)*
- *RELIGIOUS INSTITUTIONS—NATIONAL RELIGIOUS STRUCTURES SUCH AS CAMPAIGN FOR HUMAN DEVELOPMENT; LARGER REGIONAL OR DENOMINATIONAL STRUCTURES (DIOCESE; SYNOD); SUBURBAN/METRO CONGREGATIONS; INDIVIDUAL CHURCHES/TEMPLES*
- *MEMBERSHIP DUES, GRASSROOTS FUNDRAISING/SPECIAL EVENTS*
- *DIRECT MAIL/ELECTRONIC/SOCIAL MEDIA FUNDRAISING (WEB/NET)*
- *GIFTS FROM INDIVIDUALS, FACE-TO-FACE; DEFERRED/ PLANNED GIVING*
- *INCOME-PRODUCING ACTIVITIES/SALE OF MERCHANDISE*
- *FEES-FOR-SERVICE*
- *IN-KIND CONTRIBUTIONS*
- *WHO KNOWS WHAT ELSE/MYSTERY CATEGORIES*

The last item on the list confirms that it may well be incomplete. It is becoming abundantly evident that social media fundraising has come into its own, something you can verify by entering the term in a search engine. Frankly, the problem you are likely to encounter is sorting out the clutter of entries. One reasonable website as a starting point is offered in the links that follow.

By any calculation, this list offers plenty of possibilities for digging around and more than enough work to keep someone busy pursuing prospects, but there appear to be few nonprofit organizations where a staff member dedicates significant time to do this. If yours is an organization that does not fully staff resource development, including prospect research, why not consider this an area fit for fruitful work by volunteers? If volunteers often make themselves available because they want to tackle something substantive on behalf of a nonprofit organization, resource development research qualifies.

As for digging around for external resources, it is obvious that persistent diminution of money in the form of grants and contracts calls for ingenuity to keep at our mission-driven work. This may well entail scratching around for resources close to home.

Actually, this has always been an enterprising proposition, because out-of-area grant makers are likely to want to know what you've done in your own backyard before you approach them. But there is an understandable temptation to only seek out the higher profile, more active, better endowed funding sources that are front and center when you do your database research. Now, sheer necessity would seem to jolt the pursuit of local resources back into focus.

Here are the sometimes blurred bits and pieces of more localized sourcing domains:

COUNTY: General Fund; possible State Formula Allocations received for pass-through to local communities; block grants such as the community development (CDBG) and community services (CSBG) variations; possible categorical distributions for specific population groups or categories, e.g., juvenile justice; child abuse prevention.

CITY/TOWNSHIP: Program Department budgets and funds, i.e., community services, economic development/ public works, recreation department; fees imposed on operatives such as cable communication providers, land developers; local taxes.

SCHOOL DISTRICTS: General Funds; Federal Title Allocations such Title I, Elementary and Secondary Education Act; competitive categorical/discretionary funds that allow for collaboration.

PRIVATE SECTOR: Local foundations or those not local with a history of funding in your locality; local businesses/ corporations that dispense resources through various means.

These largely home-grown spheres are suggested while at the same time it is evident that current economic conditions have wreaked havoc on the availability of resources nonprofits have sought or intend to seek. The implied dampening in such a state of affairs suggests the importance of becoming all the more strategic in your efforts to reach out for assistance. So, returning to your neck of the woods, here are some questions, the answers to which are worth pursuing in service to creative tactics.

- *Are there any new sources of general local revenue, new or expanded and accessible tax receipts; earmarked fees?*
- *Are there Medicaid formula reimbursables; distributable tobacco settlement monies; unspent formula/block grant or discretionary funds?*
- *Do local hospitals or clinics distribute funds, particularly through their own foundations?*
- *Might there be new sources or categories of public sector dollars, as with previous federal stimulus funding, fed into local units of government?*
- *Is your organization taking steps to pursue relevant federal funds in conjunction with local units of government where your nonprofit status might prove advantageous? Are there public/private partnerships to promote leveraging of dollars?*
- *Is there a community foundation active in your geographic area? Is there the prospect of collaborating with local public school foundations?*
- *Is your organization attempting to generate new sources of funds that can be controlled or directed to its advantage, as in fundraising events or direct mail solicitation aimed at local community members?*

If the answers don't always present themselves when you walk through doors, this probably means walking through them again. Persistence matters, and many who confront the slings and arrows of outrageous noes would be well advised to remember this.

Next, here's a portal of a different sort that might prove useful as well. This opens up an assortment of access points, largely electronic, that in turn lead to possibilities for seeking and securing the money needed to move toward accomplishing your mission.

Resource Connections

If there is a problem to befall your intrepid pursuit of resources, it is likely to be the overwhelming volume of data that can spill out when you get going, especially if you're concentrating on what the Internet has to offer. As you know or will know, the immense power of the net is embodied in its linking capacity. One click becomes fifty. As far as this goes, you could begin with several of the entries to follow and be information rich, though not necessarily funding rich. So, this compendium represents bobbing and weaving on the ocean of information. Climb aboard.

GOOGLE
WWW.GOOGLE.COM

Start with Google, it's not the only search engine, but typing in a term as general as "nonprofit funding sources" leads to multiple millions of prospective hits.

MICHIGAN STATE UNIVERSITY LIBRARY
HTTP://STAFF.LIB.MSU.EDU/HARRIS23/GRANTS/INDEX.HTM

Michigan State University Library offers a wonderful one-stop shop for funding research. Reference forty categories under the heading, Grants and Related Resources, and these include grants for nonprofits and individuals, and funding for economic development among them. This site is also likely to steer you to the entries that follow.

THE U.S. NATIONAL ARCHIVES AND RECORDS ADMINISTRATION
WWW.ARCHIVES.GOV

The U.S. National Archives and Records Administration handles information about the Federal Register very well (Why should I read it? Who uses it? Where is it available? How do I find the information I need?) The answers to those questions will confirm why you need to consult the register in the first place—it is the fundamental source of information about federal grants. The Archives' gremlins also ace the U. S. Government Manual, the annual publication that lays out for the reader our government in all its splendor—the legislative, judicial, and executive branches, along with other related orgs, such a quasi-official agencies. For agency entries you will discover organizational charts and who runs major units by name. Also, if you want to locate your local federal depository library, where you can do federal funding research, this site will give you the address. Sweet.

FEDERAL FUNDING WEBSITE

WWW.GRANTS.GOV

FirstGov.Gov, the original site for much of the voluminous data that emanates from the feds has morphed into usa.gov. When you sign on @ usa.gov, one of the categories you will see is Benefits, Grants and Loans and shortly thereafter this leads to access to Grants.Gov. While I suspect that you may find some of the other categories on usa. gov valuable, you can go directly to grants.gov. Simply put, you will find no larger, more comprehensive data source about federal funding. You will also learn about the extent to which the feds are concentrating on the internet as the preferred medium for submitting funding proposals.

CATALOG OF FEDERAL DOMESTIC ASSISTANCE

WWW.CFDA.GOV

What displays detailed information on almost 2,300 assistance programs including the grantmaking programs of 26 federal agencies, identified by a five-digit number known as the CFDA or Catalog Number? (CFDA Number 19.801 identifies the Office of Global Women's Issues at the state department that makes grants, among other functions. Who knew?) All this and more will be found in the Catalog of Federal Domestic Assistance, that's what. This standard reference has been around since the late War on Poverty (RIP), and it's always been a good piece of work, if you know, or want to know, which federal resources might be worth pursuing for your organization.

STATE GOVERNMENT

WWW.STATELOCALGOV.NET

Don't forget state government in the scheme of resource development possibilities for your nonprofit. Federal funds get passed through state agencies, and state legislatures have been known to make money available for use by competing nonprofits. Go to the above site, and poke around your very own state.

THE FOUNDATION CENTER

WWW.FDNCENTER.ORG

The Foundation Center maintains a detailed, useful website. It covers lots of ground on which some 90,000 private grant makers stand. If you know the name of a particular private or community foundation, grantmaking public charity, or corporate giving program, this site will give you rudimentary information and, often access to several years' worth of 990 PF (annual tax return) info. The highest quality stuff about these grant makers on the formidable database the center operates is not free. Another option for you and a virtue of this website is that it will direct you to the nearest Cooperating Collection, usually a library that houses reference print materials and sit-down electronic access to the center's database. You will get access to 990 PFs at many of these places also.

990 PFs

HTTP://AG.CA.GOV/CHARITIES.PHP

The above is the link to the California State Attorney's office where just named 990 PFs for California foundations are also housed and accessible. These are worth looking into because you can learn about foundation's managers (which might include some board members), financial information, and grants made for the year of record along with the organizations receiving them. For those of you located in the other 49, or in U.S. territories, check your own Attorney General's office to see if you can dig up indigenous foundation data.

GUIDESTAR

WWW.GUIDESTAR.ORG

Guidestar belongs here simply because it purports to include information on more nonprofits than any other outfit. The emphasis is on allowing a prospective donor to assess the financial credibility of a listed organization considered for funding, including yours, if it filed a 990 tax form. Annual 990s for grantmaking foundations are accessible, though not free.

INTERNET RESOURCES

WWW.INTERNET-RESOURCES.COM/NONPROFIT

When looking for the FAQs formerly published by the Internet Nonprofit Center, I found this grab bag site with a collection of links that share a common focus on nonprofits that you might find useful.

EVALUATION WEBSITES

HTTP://CDC.GOV/EVAL/RESOURCES.HTM

WWW.ORSIMPACT.COM

These two sites, among many, seem useful because each offers a number of links to resources related to program evaluation. The reasoning for including them is to, as ever, reinforce the importance of measuring the impact of your organization's work.

CROWDFUNDING

HTTP://EN.WIKIPEDIA.ORG/WIKI/CROWDFUNDING

Finally, no list of prospective resources to support your nonprofit would be complete without a connection to the emerging realm of social media funding, aka crowdfunding. Wikipedia seems a reasonable starting point.

As much as I want to imagine that you'll find reason to read this book repeatedly to guide your work, open on your desk with dog-eared pages, the time comes when you are led back to the people who share your devotion to a certain nonprofit organization—the one pursuing resources to accomplish its mission. The Tool Kit that follows is intended to facilitate matters when you congregate.

CHAPTER NINE

KIT

- *Funding Proposal Dos and Don'ts*
- *The Elements of a Financially Healthy Nonprofit*
- *A Simple Guide to Project Planning*
- *The Keys to Developing Powerful Funding Proposals*

First among the items that follow is a think-piece about *Funding Proposal Dos and Don'ts.* Lean on it when you contemplate persuading those with available assets to become the other half of the funding partnership we have discussed.

Then comes The Elements of a Financially Healthy Nonprofit Organization. Using this to honestly assess dollars among the categories can be a daunting proposition, but not doing so is an exercise in denial. Being unschooled or unmindful about the wisdom of demonstrating or pursuing diverse resources is a dubious proposition in the crowded, highly competitive external funding arena.

Next, A Simple Guide to Project Planning—an exemplar of down-to-earth perspective about the sort of work we do in nonprofits. This document is worthy of your attention if you have the good sense to use it, let's imagine, as the guide to a conversation about a project that you are enthused about. You may be surprised by the demands of answering the questions within the grid. This underscores that developing a funding proposal requires much more than writing.

And lastly, you will encounter The Keys to Developing Powerful Funding Proposals, intended to mark your proposal building by the use of the format that is a principle feature of this book. Make copies of the pages here, or create your own version, or go to WWW.FUNCTIONALANDFUNDED.COM/TOOLKIT to download a pdf. Then do the following: Rough out your own ideas about each section to see where you are in actually compiling a sketch to become a proposal. Use your product as the basis for pulling people together for the teamwork you, by now, understand is needed to honor your product as representing your organization as a whole.

Funding Proposal Dos and Don'ts

Let's revisit the soundest definition of a funding proposal—the written version of the discussions and agreements within your organization about pursuing needed resources. This should result in a document that describes the effort for which funding is sought, along with a cogent argument for mounting it.

While it is common to focus on a particular project or program in a funding proposal, you can broaden discussions to an organization-wide purview that pinpoints all your program efforts and appropriate administration. This, in turn, might lead to developing the most attractive and challenging proposal of all, the one seeking support for general operating purposes.

The sensible suggestions to follow are intended to imprint the work of a resource development proposal writer, no matter what type of proposal emerges. Taking them to heart should assist you in avoiding the traps that lurk for those who craft these documents. Often enough the basis for a declined proposal relates to missteps that could and should have been avoided in advance of the bad news.

Begin with assumption that the people who will review your proposal are of good will, and look for quality in nonprofit organizations and their work. This suggests that you seek them out, if accessible, to ask reasonable questions prior to preparing your proposal.

Learn what you can where you can, and let your correspondent understand somewhere in the contact process that you have reviewed materials, intend to apply for funding, and need some clarification before proceeding. Such a savvy stance is likely to elevate your status in the eyes of the person handling your proposal.

Furthermore, you are likely to discover that funder-generated materials to guide your progress in writing proposals are rarely so lucid as to be self-explanatory, so you have reason to look further for clarification. Here, to make the point, is language from a grantmaking foundation: "In general, foundation grants are limited to programs and/or initiatives that have significant potential to demonstrate innovative service delivery, in support of education and entrepreneurship." At a minimum, you'd do well to learn more from the source about those modifiers, significant and innovative.

You should also be aware that funding sources, particularly grant makers, use different techniques to deal with your proposal, once received. If you discover that a face-to-face meeting to discuss your proposal is in the works, take advantage of the opportunity. Determine if your funding source counterpart will make a site visit, welcome this if so, and check what your visitor's expectations might be. Consider the wisdom of seeing to it that your side of the meeting table includes other staff, board members, community members or program participants who are prepared to be themselves when they interact with the funding rep. This is a beneficial transaction and presents the opportunity not only to reflect your organization as you would want it seen or felt, but also to listen to what your visitor has to share about the process underway.

As for face time with funding reps, don't forget that you are likely to be competing with others who want the same thing. Use your time wisely. Don't ask what the organization in focus is currently funding when there is information that at least partially explains this. This is a dead giveaway that you haven't done any homework. Far more strategic to ask for clarification of what you've already looked over.

Unfortunately, the wholesomeness of sitting down together is altogether too rare in the funding realm. Most funding organizations do not make time to meet with the someone from an outfit looking to approach them. This brings us back to the importance of your written proposal, because it may well have to stand alone as the means of representing your organization's intentions.

In your proposal, be thorough, reasonable, and positive. Don't be hesitant or quarrelsome. If unsuccessful, take steps to find out why your proposal was turned down. You won't enjoy funding declinations that far outnumber approvals. Nonetheless, you need to use them as opportunities for learning. Today's refusal; tomorrow's approval.

There is no magic in writing an effective proposal for funding, nor are there any guarantees in any single method you might choose, though you are now aware of the core framework with which to work every time your organization elects to approach a prospective benefactor.

Remember that the proposal that is truest to reflecting your organization's credibility, capability and dedication to mission accomplishment is the one you want in the hands of funding decision makers. If you think about it, such a proposal is likely to stand the best chance of being treated seriously and, even in the event it does not result in funds, it will hold up as a basis for additional efforts.

THE DOS

When Preparing a Proposal, Do:

KNOW YOUR FUNDING SOURCE. All have biases: Some favor research, others favor action; many support specific projects, a few like general support grants. Almost all will have some kind of funding track record to study. Look for written materials about policies and procedures. Look for representatives with whom to meet.

KNOW YOUR TURF. Find out if anyone else in the community is concerned about and working on the situation you're addressing, and find out what other approaches have been tried. Consider the value of coalitions with other organizations. Pay attention to the emphasis on program collaboration bandied about but seldom practiced by funders.

FOLLOW THE FORMAT. Use what a funder suggests or requires, even if accustomed to using another form or approach. Improving a funder's format courts a charge of being unresponsive, if not arrogant. This does not negate the importance of using the framework in this book to develop your proposal, although it may ultimately conform to another's protocol.

WRITE CLEARLY. Proposal reviewers usually have to read a slew of proposals in a short period. So it makes sense that they appreciate direct statements and are exasperated by cleverness or needless repetition. The best way to handle jargon and specialized acronyms that fly around in proposals is to do away with them. You are not likely to insult a reader with straightforward, explicit language. If you take five pages to say what can be said adequately in one, reviewers are likely to remember your proposal for something other than positive reasons.

WRITE SENSIBLY. The proposal should flow, with conclusions reached, not jumped at. Your organization's credibility and commitment to bringing about needed change should always shine through the words you use.

BE SPECIFIC. In short, specify numbers, sequences, and outcomes. Consider using charts to visualize timing and flow of activities, allowing for start-up and phase-in of your project when discussing your proposed approach.

BE THOROUGH especially when detailing program administration, supervision, and monitoring. Funders like to know that their money will support conscientious and capable agencies.

CRITIQUE YOUR OWN PROPOSAL before it reaches the intended funding source, and the review process begins. Proposal writers, even those good at the business, have a common failing: They become enamored of their product without reference to outside counsel, and they do not consider their work in light of the larger context in which it is proposed. Your proposal should be intelligible to any reader, especially one not familiar with your field of interest. Test yours on co-workers or friends. See if the those whose circumstances led to the proposal in the first place agree with what it says. Set aside your ego, heed their comments, and express your gratitude for their willingness to be available.

BE POSITIVE. Predicting doom if your program isn't funded, or pleading poverty, or heaping guilt on a prospective funder might work once, but will certainly be subject to the law of diminishing returns. How often can you go to the well with the old "if you don't fund us we're going to go belly up" routine? Funders like winners, and evidence of your organization's grasp of a situation and how to deal with it, essentially positing a positive attitude, is a winner's strategy.

THE DONT'S

When Preparing a Proposal, Don't:

ARGUE WITH A GRANT MAKER'S ASSUMPTIONS. If the funds are available through a Request For Proposals (RFP), it often contains a definition of a problem as the issuing organization sees it. Guidelines may also reveal a framework through which a grant maker operates. Even if you feel that these presentations are misinformed, don't take issue with them. Your countervailing knowledge will not matter in this setting. If you cannot ethically agree with a prospective funder's assumptions, avoid going after its money, and save your reforms for other forums.

PHILOSOPHIZE. A proposal for a nutrition program is no place for a speech on hunger in the Third World. Know the difference between a proposal for funding and a polemic. Avoid the implied charge that a funding refusal would mean the funder does not care about the problem. Making such a contention won't get you funded anyhow.

CONFUSE YOUR ORGANIZATION'S NEEDS WITH THE CHALLENGES THAT FACE YOUR CONSTITUENTS OR PARTICIPANTS. It is common practice to make the case that you need funds to keep your organization's doors open. It does not necessarily follow that this will redound to the benefit of the people for whom your organization exists. Making certain that you document their challenges and the need to overcome them as the basis for your proposal offers the justification for continuing to meet organizational needs.

ASSUME THE REVIEWERS KNOW THE PROBLEM OR PROGRAM. The individuals recruited to read proposals may include academicians, technicians, and just plain folks. Given this mix of possible readers, it makes sense to be specific and document the existence of challenges to be met and the capacity of your program to meet them. In all events avoid unsupported assumptions of any type, because they always raise questions that weaken a proposal.

INCLUDE SURPRISES. Examples are personnel who show up in an organizational chart or budget, but are not mentioned in the proposal narrative, or charges for categories or functions in a budget, with no prior previous references as to purpose or necessity.

PROMISE MORE THAN YOU CAN DELIVER. Resist the temptation to imagine a competitive advantage by delivering an unrealistic high level of impact or a proposed budget on the cheap and seemingly inconsistent with the scope of your intended program. In both cases, you risk your credibility either through the analysis of an experienced reviewer, or falling short of your goals should you happen to receive funds.

Remember, the effective proposal, in brief:

- *Is in the hands of the right funding source, because your research was rigorous,*
- *Gives evidence of careful detailing by your organization in its preparation,*
- *Conveys the importance of what you propose among the people who are at the heart of your mission,*
- *Includes other resources to be used with those you are requesting,*
- *Answers questions, rather than raising them.*

THE ELEMENTS OF A FINANCIALLY HEALTHY NONPROFIT

SOURCE	AMOUNT	% TOTAL BUDGET
Individual		
Membership Dues		
Direct Mail/Email/Social		
Special Events		
Income Producing Devices		
Workplace Solicitation		
Planned Giving/Bequests		
Private Sector		
Corporations		
Foundations		
Religious Institutions		
Grantmaking Public Charities, Civic, and Professional Organizations		
Federated Giving		
Public Sector Institutions		
Local Government		
State Government		
Federal Government		
TOTAL		

A SIMPLE GUIDE TO PROJECT PLANNING

WHY will we do what we intend to do?

Making the Case

Who are the participants for the project or program?

What are the circumstances, situations or challenges that motivate us to want to get into action?

Consequences of acting? Not acting?

- For the participants
- For the rest of us as neighbors and employers
- Customers, Parents, Families, Vendors, Taxpayers, Citizens

HOW are we going to do what we're going to do?

Blueprint

What are the steps in the plan of action?

What is the timeline for accomplishing the work of the plan?

Do we have the skills, experiences and abilities to do what's required?

How will we keep track of the work as it is being done?

How will we define and evaluate the success of the work as it's being done and when it's completed?

This four-column grid is a guide to thinking through and developing the steps for an effort that you think is important, and consistent with your mission as an organization or community.

WHAT will it take to do what we're going to do?

Price Tag

Salaries and Wages, Benefits, Occasional Labor, Facilities, Equipment Supplies, Services, Technical Assistance, Scholarships Stipends Fees and Licenses, Publications, Travel, Construction, Renovation, Rehabilitation, Replacement, Audio-visuals, Consumables, Insurance, Professional Advice, Utilities, Communications, Awards and recognition, Celebration, Recreation, Decoration

WHERE will we find the resources to do what we're going to do?

Income/In-Kind

What resources of our own do we have to use to cover necessary costs?

Savings, Earned money, Surplus, Fees, Tuition In-Kind

What other sources can we approach to raise the rest of the needed $$$?

Individuals, including Board, Staff, Family members, Friends, Participants, Former participants

Professional and Civic Orgs.

Clubs, Membership Assocs.

THE KEYS TO DEVELOPING POWERFUL FUNDING PROPOSALS

Use these keys ***ON YOUR OWN OR AS YOU COLLABORATE*** with others, and jot down any thoughts or ideas in the notes sections below.

If you're ***BRAINSTORMING***, consider giving everyone time to write down ideas on sticky notes, then review ideas together as a group. And remember to be supportive and encouraging during the process.

Discuss, deliberate, and develop the **CASE FOR NEEDED CHANGE**

Focus on the circumstances confronting the community or people for whom your organization exists. However you define these, e.g., barriers, or challenges, or unrealized opportunities, the point is that you are describing diminished quality of life. This forms the basis for your entire proposal.

KEY POINT: Their issues, not your organization's—keep your organization out of here.

Work on **DEFINING PARTICIPANT SUCCESS**

Evolving from the preceding section, this is where you describe needed change in the form of participant success, using specific, measurable terms. Notice that this must precede the description of your intended program.

KEY POINT: Participant-centered results, not organizational activities. Keep your organization out of here.

Work out the **PROGRAM STRATEGY**

Provide the details of your program strategy, staffing and management to bring about participant success. Explain why you've selected this approach.

KEY POINT: Activities leading to impact previously described.

Wrestle with and develop the

EVALUATION METHODS

These should serve to monitor your program as it unfolds, allowing for change as needed, and verify the level of impact in your proposed outcomes once the program has been established.

KEY POINT: Protecting organizational credibility and the investment through voluntary accountability.

Feature the quality and credibility of your organization in the **INTRODUCTION TO THE APPLICANT FOR FUNDING**

You want to impress the reader and remember that your organization is competing with others in pursuing resources.

KEY POINT: Know your organization well enough to describe it convincingly.

Add in other resources, either cash or in-kind, to demonstrate **BLENDING RESOURCES**

This represents tangible commitment to your proposed project and serves as an inducement to fund it.

KEY POINT: It takes resources to get resources.

Protect a funder's investment with plans for **MAINTAINING CONTINUITY**

You understand that projects often have a life beyond proposed funding, and want to demonstrate concern for how future costs will be underwritten.

KEY POINT: Diversified assets over time are always important when it comes to putting resource development into proper perspective.

Develop the **BUDGET AND BUDGET NARRATIVE**

This is where you articulate project costs associated with the Program Strategy, and the items included when the proposal describes blending resources. Use a narrative to justify and reconcile the numbers.

KEY POINT: Connect the budget to the rest of the proposal, especially the program strategy.

Capsulize the proposal in a **SUMMARY**

This is a thumbnail sketch that sets up your proposal when it is repackaged into the presentation format. It will prove useful in building pre-proposal documents such as Letters of Inquiry favored by some grant makers.

KEY POINT: A mini-proposal will come in handy as a marketing device.

Once the developmental process has been completed within your organization, you will turn your attention to putting all the concepts together in a way that will facilitate the reading of your funding proposal. You will repack these elements to present the proposal. Your three-part package out the door is likely to look like this in the order displayed.

The Cover Letter will be followed by the full proposal, followed by the attachments. The exception will be when a funder tells you otherwise and supplies its own format.

COVER LETTER

PROPOSAL

- *Summary*
- *Introduction to the applicant organization*
- *Case for needed change*
- *Participant-generated outcomes*
- *Proposed plan of action*
- *Evaluation methods other Resources continuity*
- *Budget and budget narrative*

ATTACHMENTS

As you read and reread this book and decide to use what it offers to guide your resource development efforts, keep the following perspective in mind. May you and yours succeed in accomplishing the mission that drew you together in the first place. That way you can regroup and reinvigorate your commitment to help other people help themselves secure a higher quality of life, secure in the knowledge that you just succeeded, and that there's bound to be more work to do.

Acknowledgements and Dedications

I have the great good fortune to hang around with a bunch of people who share the wise tenet for living that asserts: I can't, we can. So it was with the creation of this book: I couldn't, we have. I had it in mind for a long time to pull together a book based on my many years as a staff member, consultant, and trainer working among those who make it their business to pursue resources to support their nonprofit organizations.

So I got enough gumption to pull together two previous versions of such a publication of which there is plenty of history, the only important remnant of which is that I have finally arrived at the book I always wanted to get out there, Functional and Funded, Securing Your Nonprofit's Assets From The Inside-Out. Your hands and eyes are on it one way or another if you're picking up these words. So, my first acknowledgement is to you for that.

As for some very significant others who have led up to this creation, there are a bunch.

Michael Potts was my first editor, Maria Goodwin, my second, and each steered me through the back and forth of building the predecessors to this volume for which they get my thanks.

Then there was Torrey Douglas whose work I had seen on her website Lemon Fresh Design. She brought her patience, inquisitiveness, and creativity to bear on what this itinerant was looking for. This culminated in her brilliant design of the original cover of the book after listening to me share my sense of what distinguishes legitimate nonprofit organizations.

And now, this author is the beneficiary of the extraordinary work of Anya Farquhar. An exceptional talent, she has pulled together the team responsible for crafting what I previously labeled the book I always wanted to get out there, here and now.

There were also my years of traveling the public service path decorated by encounters with a slew of remarkable people. These very same years have undoubtedly conspired to impede my ability to fully acknowledge every soul to whom I owe a debt of gratitude for being part of this splendid journey. So let me dance around this by beginning with heartfelt thanks for the opportunity to be with and learn from all the folks who toil at the doorstep and enter our nonprofit edifice. It's only fitting that this book be dedicated to you since its substance is derived from much of what we shared when together.

Hubie Williamson, who introduced me to an uncommonly wise strength as a community activist, reinforcing the quality of resilience among the people for whom he advocated, a characteristic I continue to look for when working among nonprofits.

Larry McDonough, a career civil servant that left us far too early, who always imprinted me with his way of getting things done, never losing sight of the people we were working together to serve.

P. Bertrand Phillips, who hired me at the firm he had founded, to become a faculty member at the Navy's Race Relations Education School, an experience that embedded social justice in my frame of the nonprofit, public benefit sector where I get to work.

Norton Kiritz, no longer with us, far too early, because he saw something in me that motivated him to make me a trainer for The Grantsmanship Center, his living legacy. The resultant experience shares equal billing with the next as a standard for my work.

Jack Shakely, who made me part of the emergence of the foundation he headed, an experience that influences my professional efforts to this day.

Jan Stohr, the founding director of the management support organization through which much of my training and consulting has flourished.

Then there were my children, Matthew, Tim, Aimy and Emma, grown adults now, and their mother, Susan Aguilera, who were there from the get-go, not always in the easiest of times.

Finally, more than any of these remarkable individuals, I trust you will understand that my devotion to my life partner, Sandra Jean Baldocchi, knows no bounds. I am grateful for her wondrous forbearance and love while sharing life on life's terms with me.

About the Author

Harvey B. Chess freely admits not knowing what he was getting into in 1965 when a recruiter for a new federal agency beguiled him by stating that the organization's mission was to eliminate poverty in this country.

He'd also freely admit that the experience was his touchstone and a rare privilege because it marked the consonance between the core values he developed and his work since then.

Such work has always been with and among people in nonprofit organizations as a well-regarded trainer, peripatetic consultant, and fitful volunteer—and now less nomadically, as an author.

Much of what he has come to learn, practice, and cherish is now embodied in this book. A great deal of that background was couched in the ever-alluring arena of grantseeking, including years of presenting an acclaimed workshop on that subject.

Chess has it in mind to continue writing, while also promoting the book, by blogging on his two websites, one personal, WWW.HARVEYBCHESS.COM, the other professional, WWW.FUNCTIONALANDFUNDED.COM.

Meanwhile, he can be found as a grateful soul sharing his life one day at a time with a beloved partner among the redwoods and near the Pacific in Mendocino County, California.

HARVEY B. CHESS

Resident Ruminant, THE WOODS, LITTLE RIVER, CA
The FTF Group, LITTLE RIVER, CA
Nonprofit Resource Center, SACRAMENTO, CA
Sierra Health Foundation, SACRAMENTO, CA
Community Network For Children & Families, GRASS VALLEY, CA
Stanislaus County Office of Education Healthy Start, MODESTO, CA
Sinte Gleska University, ROSEBUD, SD
Indian Law Resource Center, HELENA, MT
Piegan Institute, BROWNING, MT
Washiw Wagayay Mangal, GARDNERVILLE, NV
Lannan Foundation, SANTA FE, NM
Hawaii Department of Health, HONOLULU & HILO, HI
Taos Valley Acequia Association, TAOS, NM
New Mexico Department of Health, LAS CRUCES, NM
New Mexico Community Foundation, SANTA FE, NM
CA Wellness Foundation, SAN FRANCISCO, CA
The Life & Peace Institute, UPPSALA, SWEDEN
SALUS/Pacific Institute for Evaluation, WASHINGTON, DC
National Training Associates, SEBASTOPOL, CA
Touchstone Center, ALBION, CA
Telecommunications Education Trust, SAN FRANCISCO, CA
The Tides Foundation, SAN FRANCISCO, CA
Sonoma County Foundation, SANTA ROSA, CA
University of New Mexico Hospital, ALBUQUERQUE, NM
Tucson Community Foundation, TUCSON, AZ
Episcopal Migration Ministries, NEW YORK, NY
Church World Service, NEW YORK, NY
Grants Program of Trinity Parish, NEW YORK, NY
James Irvine Foundation, SAN FRANCISCO, CA
Project Open Hand, SAN FRANCISCO, CA
UCLA Extension, WESTWOOD, CA
Art Institute of So. CA, LAGUNA BEACH, CA
Orange County Community Development Council, SANTA ANA, CA
Southwest Border AIDS Collaborative, LOS ANGELES, CA
National Community AIDS Partnership, RICHMOND, VA; LOS ANGELES, CA
California Community Foundation, LOS ANGELES, CA

Cancer Support Community, SAN FRANCISCO, CA
The University of Alaska, FAIRBANKS, AK
Tacoma Community House, TACOMA, WA
College of The Redwoods, EUREKA, CA
Stanford University Hospital, STANFORD, CA
Truckee Associates, SAN FRANCISCO, CA
The Grantsmanship Center, LOS ANGELES, CA
La Cooperativa, SACRAMENTO, CA
Office of Navajo Economic Opportunity, FT. DEFIANCE, AZ
Laney College, OAKLAND, CA
One-To-One, NEW YORK, NY
CA Coalition of Children, Youth & Families, SAN FRANCISCO, CA
Junior League, St., JOSEPH, MO
Michigan Technological University, HOUGHTON, MI
Department of Health, Education & Welfare, WASHINGTON, DC
Indochina Refugee Rask Force, WASHINGTON, DC
ACTION, Region II, NEW YORK, NY
Curber Associates, WASHINGTON, DC
Navy Race Relations School, KEY WEST, FL
The Pentagon, Arlington, VA
Navy Human Goals Program, MILLINGTON, TN
National Institutes of Health, WASHINGTON, DC
ACTION, Region III, WASHINGTON, DC
Washington School of Psychiatry, DC BGE Consultants, ARLINGTON, VA
OAR, Fairfax, VA NACO, WASHINGTON, DC
Pearl St Neighborhood House, WATERBURY, CT
Multi-Racial Corp., WASHINGTON, DC
TRISED, NEW YORK, NY
MAP, Manpower Assistance Project, WASHINGTON, DC
Community Action for Greater MIDDLETOWN, CT
New Opportunities for WATERBURY, CT
Duncan-Medical Center YMCA, Chicago, IL
Office of Economic Opportunity, REGION V

Many branches climbed on the tree of professional experience since stumbling into the nonprofit sector in 1965.

CPSIA information can be obtained
at www.ICGtesting.com
'inted in the USA
'V01n0955050818
'S

9 780996 314718